WITH GOD
I WILL NOT FEAR

A 90-DAY DEVOTIONAL

Chosen

a division of Baker Publishing Group
Minneapolis, Minnesota

© 2023 by Baker Publishing Group

Published by Chosen Books
Minneapolis, Minnesota
www.chosenbooks.com

Chosen Books is a division of
Baker Publishing Group, Grand Rapids, Michigan

Printed in China

Library of Congress Cataloging-in-Publication Data
Title: With God I will not fear : a 90-day devotional.
Description: Minneapolis, Minnesota : Chosen Books, a division of Baker Publishing Group, [2023] | Series: With God
Identifiers: LCCN 2022028314 | ISBN 9780800762711 (imitation leather) | ISBN 9781493437689 (ebook)
Subjects: LCSH: Fear—Religious aspects—Christianity—Miscellanea. | Fear—Biblical teaching. | Fear—Prayers and devotions.
Classification: LCC BV4908.5 .W58 2023 | DDC 201/.615246—dc23/eng/20220815
LC record available at https://lccn.loc.gov/2022028314

Written by Deb Borman, Yolandita Colón, David P. French, Maurice Gavin, Nikki Harris, Hope Johnson and Susanna Crook

Cover design by Studio Gearbox

Baker Publishing Group publications use paper produced from sustainable forestry practices and post-consumer waste whenever possible.

23   24   25   26   27   28   29   7   6   5   4   3   2   1

CONTENTS

INTRODUCTION

Whatever you are facing, with God, you do not need to fear!

The Bible records the words *do not fear, do not be afraid* or something similar over one hundred times in Scripture, reminding us that in even the most terrifying of situations, we can have courage and confidence as we rest in the presence of the God who loves, leads and protects us. This perfect love of Jesus Christ drives out fear (1 John 4:18), empowering us to face our fears with holy boldness.

This book looks at ninety of those instances in Scripture where God or another person emboldened someone by saying "Do not be afraid!" This devotional is designed to illuminate the courage and confidence you can have amid every type of fear you experience—from anxiety about the future to fear of failure, from terror of the evil in the world to fear of what others think. As you read, you will be reminded of the bold new creation you are in Christ, encouraged to embrace this truth and challenged to act fearlessly, confident that He will never leave you nor forsake you (Deuteronomy 31:8).

Each day's reading is two short pages that contain the following:

- A powerful, courage-filled Scripture to read purposefully and prayerfully. The Word of God is able to encourage and strengthen.
- An inspirational meditation you can read in under two minutes.
- A personalized reflective question and a prayer to help you talk to God about what you have read.
- An affirmative declaration to repeat throughout your day, which will help lock in a hopeful truth.
- A practical action that will encourage you to step out in courageous faith with the help of the Holy Spirit.

May the words in this book strengthen your faith, open your eyes to God's love and faithfulness and empower you to live your life in light of the truth that with God, you do not need to fear.

1 Your Shield and Reward

> After these things the word of the LORD came to Abram in a vision, saying, "Do not be afraid, Abram. I am your shield, your exceedingly great reward."
>
> Genesis 15:1 NKJV

When you have been afraid, have you ever looked past what God has done and focused instead on the logistical uncertainties of His promises?

Despite clear promises from God, supernatural experiences and victories in battle, Abram still experienced fear regarding his seemingly heirless future. God had previously promised "offspring" who would come through Abram. These words from the mouth of God should have silenced Abram's line of questioning regarding a natural-born heir. Yet Abram was still troubled at the thought of his household and wealth being left to a servant.

As we often do today, Abram unsettled himself by focusing on the uncertainty rather than the promises God Himself made face-to-face. God's antidote for any fear that Abram or we, his descendants by faith, would ever confront is enclosed in the revelation that He is both our "shield" and our "exceedingly great reward." God offered Himself as a permanent inheritance to all those who through faith are partakers of the promise made to Abram and later Jesus (see Romans 9:7–9).

You, like the father of your faith, Abraham, can terminate the tendency to fear by focusing on God as your "shield" and "exceedingly great reward."

▶ **REFLECT** What does it look like for God to be my shield?

▶ **PRAY** God, help me to see the power and size of the shield You are in my life. Remind me of all the biblical accounts where You overcame Israel's and even Jesus' enemies and led Your people to safety despite impossible odds. Help me see that nothing in this life can outweigh Your protection.

▶ **DECLARE** God is my shield and great reward.

▶ **ACT** Who around you needs God as a shield today? Reach out to them, encourage them or offer to pray for them.

God Hears My Cry

> And God heard the voice of the boy, and the angel of God called to Hagar from heaven and said to her, "What troubles you, Hagar? Fear not, for God has heard the voice of the boy where he is."
>
> Genesis 21:17 ESV

You may occasionally come close to giving in to fear and giving up, but the account of Hagar and Ishmael should convince you never to do that.

Consider this rather desperate story and take courage. Abram and Sarai were married for many years but were childless. Sarai persuaded Abram to have a child with her maid, Hagar, and they had a son named Ishmael.

Thirteen years later, Abraham and Sarah had a miracle child named Isaac. When Ishmael was cruel toward Isaac, Sarah drove him and Hagar into the wilderness. Hagar gave up all hope when their water ran out. It seems she had forgotten how the Lord had already rescued her before in the wilderness (see Genesis 16:11).

The Bible says preteen Ishmael cried in utter desperation, and God heard him. Possibly he was crying out to the God of his father, Abraham, since surely Ishmael had witnessed him praying and making sacrifices to the Lord. The angel then spoke to Hagar, asking her what was wrong and urging her not to be afraid, because her son's prayer had been heard.

Whatever you may face today, rather than fear, be assured that your simple cry will be heard. God, who heard Ishmael's cry, will hear yours.

▶ **REFLECT** How has God answered my cries in the past?

▶ **PRAY** Father, I thank You for Your Word, which teaches me of Your mercies toward Hagar, an Egyptian servant, and her son, Ishmael. As You heard Ishmael, hear my heart's cry today and answer me in those matters that trouble me. Let me realize that I don't need eloquent words or great knowledge of You, but only simple and sincere faith.

▶ **DECLARE** The Lord hears my cries.

▶ **ACT** Go to a private place and cry out before the Lord, allowing yourself to pour out your heart without censoring yourself.

3 The Blessing of God's Presence

> And the LORD appeared to him the same night and said, "I am the God of your father Abraham; do not fear, for I am with you. I will bless you and multiply your descendants, for the sake of My servant Abraham."
>
> Genesis 26:24 NASB

Do you have confidence that God is with you? The patriarch Isaac is a great example of how confidence in God's presence empowers you to face your fear.

Isaac was a miracle child born when his father was one hundred and his mother ninety. His life wasn't easy, but God was with him, and he seemed to know it. At one point, there was a drought, and he moved locations to stay fed. God blessed him so that he sowed in a famine and reaped a hundredfold harvest! He must have realized that his father's God was with him—and so did the Philistine king, who pushed him out of the city.

In the countryside, Isaac found several wells that local men contested until he finally found one to which he could lay claim. Noting that God must have made room for him, Isaac built an altar to thank the Lord. During so many trials,

Isaac kept his composure, confident that God's presence was with him, just as it had been with his father, Abraham.

In the same way, God is with you to help you endure testing and face your fears. Like Isaac, be confident that God's presence is with you every step of the way.

▶ **REFLECT** How has God been with others I know, and how can that encourage me that God will be with me too?

▶ **PRAY** Lord, whatever my circumstances are today, I choose to keep my composure and trust You, giving thanks for every small victory and being assured that You are with me. May I take courage from Your work in the lives of others and know that You are at work in mine.

▶ **DECLARE** God is with me wherever I go.

▶ **ACT** Visualize the next fear you need to face and determine how you will act according to the confidence that God is with you.

4 Abundant Grace

He replied, "Peace to you, do not be afraid. Your God and
the God of your father has put treasure in your sacks for
you. I received your money." Then he brought Simeon out
to them.

Genesis 43:23 ESV

Imagine receiving a message that the entire amount you
paid in taxes this year was being returned to you with no
explanation. Would you feel nervous, afraid or uncertain?

Joseph's brothers undoubtedly felt a range of unsettling
emotions when they opened their grain sacks and found
their purchase price still in their possession rather than in
the hands of Egypt's highest-ranking government official
and grain seller: Joseph. Their consciences had already con-
victed them (see Genesis 42:21–22), and their guilt made any
future misfortune well deserved.

Yet, through Joseph, God was at work, again showing His
underserved favor and mercy to Joseph's brothers.

God offers us the same today. Before His perfect standards of justice, we are all guilty as charged because nothing
is hidden from Him. Yet, despite His full knowledge of our
willful disobedience and our conscious trespasses against

His standards of righteousness, He offers us not only forgiveness, but access to His family as joint-heirs with Jesus (see Romans 8:16–18).

As you cast the whole of your cares upon Him, His love and mercy deposit your shortcomings into a sea of forgetfulness, never to be remembered again. It is for this reason that we can have joy without fear.

▶ **REFLECT** When have I experienced God's unmerited favor and mercy in my life?

▶ **PRAY** God, show me the magnitude of Your forgiveness and grace so I can draw closer to You and become more aware of who I am in You. I bring all my flaws, mistakes and willful sins to Your feet in exchange for Your loving grace and mercy, which Jesus provided through His sacrifice on the cross at Calvary.

▶ **DECLARE** God's mercy is abundant in my life.

▶ **ACT** Look for evidence of God's grace and mercy in your life today. Then share what you see with a friend.

5 Courage for Your Calling

> God spoke to Israel in the visions of the night, and said, "Jacob, Jacob!" He said, "Here I am." He said, "I am God, the God of your father. Don't be afraid to go down into Egypt, for there I will make of you a great nation."
>
> Genesis 46:2–3 WEB

What do you believe God has called you to do that requires courage?

Jacob's life had been filled with uncertainty, disappointment and tragedy, but also supernatural success. His father, Isaac, was also confronted with a time of famine and had the opportunity to go down to Egypt until the famine subsided (see Genesis 26:2–5). Yet his staying in the Promised Land in obedience to God resulted in blessing, so it is understandable why God would have given Jacob the confidence to live out his remaining years in Egypt.

God wants to speak to you as He did to Abraham, Isaac and Jacob. He sees the future in ways you cannot begin to imagine, and with His direction, you can navigate the uncertainties ahead with unshakable confidence.

If hearing God's voice sounds far-fetched or impossible, simply take a moment to get quiet and listen to the impressions on your heart. Ask Him to reveal His calling on your life in this season and to destroy any fear that may be holding you back from moving toward where He is leading you.

After weighing whatever you hear against the wise counsel of Scripture and godly leaders who love you, take action.

▶ **REFLECT** What is God calling me to do that fear is attempting to disqualify me from embracing?

▶ **PRAY** God, thank You for revealing Your calling for my life and the next steps I should take. Help me to hear Your words of comfort and direction so I can do exactly what You have asked of me, regardless of whether it is out of my emotional or physical comfort zone.

▶ **DECLARE** God gives me courage to fulfill my calling.

▶ **ACT** Write down what you feel God is calling you to do and then write down any fears you need to overcome to fully embrace His direction.

6 Stay Calm

> But Moses told the people, "Don't be afraid. Just stand still and watch the LORD rescue you today. The Egyptians you see today will never be seen again. The LORD himself will fight for you. Just stay calm."
>
> Exodus 14:13–14 NLT

Do you find it difficult to stay calm when adversity comes? Have you ever felt tempted to *help* God because He was not moving fast enough? Life is difficult, but trusting God is key during hard times.

The Israelites had to learn to trust God in their scariest time. It was crucial to stay calm and expectant as God's power saved them from their enemies. God desired to show Himself to them so they could receive a deeper understanding of who He was. They had never seen God's power the way they saw it displayed that day. Can you imagine their awe as they walked on dry ground between the water walls of the Red Sea?

God wants to display His power over your situation as you stand still while He fights for you. However, standing still takes a huge amount of trust. You can't trust someone you don't know. This is why spending quiet times in God's presence and meditating on His Word is crucial.

The more you know Him, the more you will trust Him. And the more you trust Him, the more you will be able to stay calm as you watch *Him* overcome your fears.

► **REFLECT** Why is it challenging to stay calm during troubled times?

► **PRAY** Father God, thank You for Your faithful Word. Help me grow my trust in You. Empower me to stay calm and see Your glorious power in action during difficult times. Lord, help me overcome my fears in the midst of trouble. Father, show me Your glory and give me a deeper understanding of who You are.

► **DECLARE** God makes me calm in adversity.

► **ACT** Turn on some instrumental worship music and practice staying calm in His presence as you meditate on His Word.

7 Fear God, but Don't Be Afraid

> "Don't be afraid," Moses answered them, "for God has come in this way to test you, and so that your fear of him will keep you from sinning!"
>
> Exodus 20:20 NLT

Have you ever interpreted a circumstance in life to mean that God doesn't like you or is punishing you? Or have you experienced the power of God's creation and felt extremely small and helpless?

In this Old Testament Scripture, we read words like *test* and *fear*, which could lead us to conclude that God is the angry judge on high waiting to condemn us. Yet, in the Gospels, we learn from Jesus that God is a loving Father who welcomes us as the father did the Prodigal Son (see Luke 15:11–32).

God, who is perfect and holy, never changes, but He has changed *us* so He can have true fellowship with us. This change has so affected us in His eyes that we are thereafter referred to in the New Testament as the "righteousness of

God in Christ Jesus," as a result of Jesus' all-encompassing sacrifice on the cross as our sin substitute.

In Jesus, all your sins have been paid for. The need to fear God's punishment has been replaced by a pathway, paved by Christ's blood, to the base of God's throne, where you can always receive help in your time of need.

▶ **REFLECT** How do I balance understanding both the fear of the Lord and God's love for me?

▶ **PRAY** God, help me to fully understand how Jesus' life, death and resurrection have changed how You see me and how I can see You. Help me come boldly to Your throne in my time of need. Show me Your holiness and righteousness so I can appropriately fear You while also growing in my understanding of how much You love me.

▶ **DECLARE** God's perfect love casts out my fear.

▶ **ACT** Help someone you love who is in need today, while reflecting on God's love and desire to help you in your own time of need.

8　A Good Night's Sleep

> "I will give you peace in the land, and you will be able to sleep with no cause for fear. I will rid the land of wild animals and keep your enemies out of your land."
>
> Leviticus 26:6 NLT

A good night's sleep is a precious gift, giving you strength for the next day's tasks. But how can you fight the worries and fears that so often interrupt your rest?

A child sleeping soundly in a mother's arms conveys a picture of complete trust and contentment. Whatever our age, something in us longs for such perfect rest. But life gets complicated as we get older. We face constant decisions, responsibilities and stress. We get blindsided by sudden loss or abandonment from people we trusted. Even when things are going well, we fear what may await us in the future.

All these fears can rob us of the peaceful sleep God promises to His people. Thankfully, we have a heavenly Father who fully understands these fears. He doesn't reprimand us or simply tell us not to be afraid. Instead, He promises to give us peace and take action against whatever frightens us. We don't know how He will accomplish His promises, but we know we can trust His Word.

Do not fear anything or anyone that may seem to threaten you. Lie down with confidence and peace tonight, trusting that God is with you, keeping you from all harm.

▶ **REFLECT** What has been keeping me awake at night that I need to hand over to God?

▶ **PRAY** Dear Father, I find it hard to sleep when my mind is full of fears and the troubles of my day. Sometimes I don't even know what I am afraid of. Thank You for promising to give me peace. I will sleep tonight trusting that You are with me and will take care of me, protecting me against any threat.

▶ **DECLARE** God gives me peace to sleep without fear.

▶ **ACT** Before bed tonight, write down any reason you are feeling anxious. Tell Jesus you trust Him with those cares, then rest, knowing He is taking care of those needs and will give you peaceful sleep.

9 Enemies Defeated

"Only don't rebel against Yahweh, neither fear the people of the land; for they are bread for us. Their defense is removed from over them, and Yahweh is with us. Don't fear them."

Numbers 14:9 WEB

It takes the eyes of faith to see what God is doing behind the scenes, especially when you have a big enemy standing right in front of you! Joshua and Caleb had a different spirit in them and were able to see God and reject fear (see Numbers 14:24). What about you?

The ten unbelieving spies described the Canaanites as mighty monsters, and the Israelites who had not personally seen them were alarmed. But Caleb and Joshua were able to look at the inhabitants of Canaan through the eyes of faith and see them as bread—an everyday substance to be consumed.

Instead of seeing the strength of the enemy, Joshua and Caleb saw a mighty God who was with them and had already gone before them to remove the defense of the enemy. They saw a people whose protection had been removed by God, making Canaan and its people like an open banquet table for them to enjoy, a new manna whereby God would sustain them.

Whatever God has called you to do and wherever He is leading you to go, choose to believe that He can turn your greatest opposition into a decisive victory.

▶ **REFLECT** What "enemies" are occupying the "land" God has given to me to occupy?

▶ **PRAY** Open my eyes, Lord, to see the land You have provided for me. Help me to cultivate it and keep a different spirit within me. I want to be one who hears Your voice and believes Your Word. Lord, fill me with the Holy Spirit to move forward and boldly take the land You have promised to me.

▶ **DECLARE** Every enemy is defeated by God, who is with me.

▶ **ACT** Take a step forward into an area where you know God is calling you.

10   Do Not Fear Anger

"Hear the cases of those who are poor as well as those who are rich. Don't be afraid of anyone's anger, for the decision you make is God's decision."

Deuteronomy 1:17 NLT

Have you ever feared making a tough, yet right, decision, one that would make someone happy and another feeling that they were treated unfairly?

Moses knew the power and burdens of leadership from his time as a child in Pharaoh's household. He also knew the human tendency to allow power to corrupt otherwise moral decisionmakers. After walking with the all-seeing and all-knowing One, it was clear that any system of justice would have to be rooted in honesty and integrity, measured by God's standards rather than people's approval.

God's decisions are rooted in both His love for us and His righteousness. He is no respecter of persons, but instead He has bound Himself to uphold His own Word—regardless of whether humans approve of His ways.

It only makes sense that we should be imitators of our heavenly Father as we make decisions that bring glory to His name. The decisions God calls us to make will not please everyone, but we should not allow the fear of others' anger to tempt us toward indecision.

When God calls you to make an unpopular decision, find your courage in *His* approval as you act in faith. No matter how others respond, He will reward your obedience.

▶ **REFLECT** When have I felt pressured to compromise to avoid the potential unpleasant retaliation against a right decision?

▶ **PRAY** Father, thank You for revealing truth to me in every circumstance. Help me to recognize my sensitivity to the opinions of others so I can anchor myself in Your Word and Your ways. Help me to stand immovable once I am clear on Your direction so that my decisions find favor with You, regardless of earthly consequences.

▶ **DECLARE** God gives me the wisdom and strength to make good decisions.

▶ **ACT** Review an upcoming decision, ask God for His perspective so you can stick with His direction in the face of opposition and make a plan to respond accordingly.

11 Activate God's Promises

"See, the LORD your God has set the land before you. Go up, take possession, as the LORD, the God of your fathers, has told you. Do not fear or be dismayed."

Deuteronomy 1:21 ESV

What broken promise have you experienced? Even in this world filled with unfaithful people, there is great news: God never breaks His promises because He is truly faithful.

God had promised the people of Israel that they would possess a land of blessings, but they had a hard time believing they could conquer it. Moses, their leader, reminded them of the promise God had made and encouraged them to believe without fear or dismay. Now was the time to step up and take possession of the Promised Land.

However, for the promise to be activated and unleashed, they needed to see through the eyes of God's faithfulness, believe in His promise and take action to possess the land.

God wants the same for you. God does not lie, and He will never break His promises to you. When you take *fearless action* in faith to activate and possess what God has promised you, God empowers you to win the battle.

God will activate His promises over you when you believe and take action to possess what He has given you. You can be fearless as you step out in faith!

▶ **REFLECT** What intimidates me from taking action to possess God's promises?

▶ **PRAY** Father God, thank You for Your faithfulness to people throughout history and Your faithfulness in my life today. Open the eyes of my heart to see You and the greatness of Your promises. Strengthen my faith as I trust in Your promises over my life. Empower me to take fearless action to activate, conquer and possess Your promises today.

▶ **DECLARE** God's promises will come to pass!

▶ **ACT** Write down a promise God has made to you and take a fearless step of action toward it today.

12 | God Is Fighting for You

> "Then I said to you, 'Do not be in dread or afraid of them.
> The LORD your God who goes before you will himself fight
> for you, just as he did for you in Egypt before your eyes.'"
>
> Deuteronomy 1:29–30 ESV

You learn someone's true character when he or she comes through for you in times of trouble. Have you ever had someone stand up for you or fight on your behalf?

God had shown His great power and mercy to the tribes of Israel—over one million people—delivering them miraculously from a harsh Egyptian pharaoh and destroying those who pursued them. Patiently, the Lord led His people through the wilderness in a pillar of fire by night and a cloud by day, showing the way to a better land and providing for every need along the way.

But the people of Israel did not trust God. According to Moses, they did not trust Him because they did not remember how "in the wilderness . . . the LORD . . . carried [them], as a man carries his son" (Deuteronomy 1:31 ESV). Because they did not remember His faithfulness in the past, fear caused them to miss out on the good land God desired to give them.

When frightening circumstances tempt you to shrink back from trusting God, remember those situations when He proved Himself faithful, did the impossible or gave grace to see you through. Trust that He Himself will faithfully fight for you, no matter what challenge you may face.

▶ **REFLECT** When have I experienced God fighting for me?

▶ **PRAY** Precious Savior, thank You for keeping Your promises to me throughout my life. When I feel afraid, help me remember the ways You have come through for me in the past. Lead me through the wilderness, fighting my enemies. I trust that, whatever is ahead of me, You have good plans for me and will provide everything I need.

▶ **DECLARE** God is faithfully fighting for me.

▶ **ACT** Listen to a song with lyrics that remind you of God's faithfulness to fight on your behalf. Let the words encourage you to remember that He who helped you in the past will help you today.

13 Speak Truth to Yourself

> You may say to yourselves, "These nations are stronger than we are. How can we drive them out?" But do not be afraid of them; remember well what the LORD your God did to Pharaoh and to all Egypt.
>
> Deuteronomy 7:17–18 NIV

Fear increases when you reflect on the size of the trial you're facing. It feeds off thoughts of the trial's magnitude, but it starves when you focus on the powerful God who is with you in it!

When Moses spoke to Israel of the Promised Land, he discerned that their focus was on the strength of the nations they were to drive out. Fearful Israel had forgotten the most vital part of the equation—the God of the universe was with them. Moses implored them to meditate on how God had already delivered them from a nation that was far stronger than they were. Just as God had miraculously saved them from the strength of Egypt, so would He save them when they followed Him into the Promised Land.

Our innermost thoughts matter greatly in the battle against fear. When we tell ourselves of our inability to overcome our trials, fear paralyzes us, but when we tell ourselves of God's power to do the impossible, He emboldens us to act courageously.

Fix your eyes on the One who has unlimited power, replacing thoughts of your weakness with the truth that God is stronger than any trial you face.

▶ **REFLECT** What truth about God can I remind myself of to fight my fearful thoughts?

▶ **PRAY** Father God, reveal any lies I am telling myself that are keeping me enslaved to fear and replace them with truth. You are the Way, the Truth and the Life—by the power of the Holy Spirit, empower me to walk in Your truth as I live a life defined not by fear, but by trust.

▶ **DECLARE** God is stronger than any trial I face.

▶ **ACT** Just as Moses pointed Israel to God's strength when they were afraid, remind someone—especially someone facing a trial—of God's power by sharing something He has done in the past.

Our Great and Awesome God

> "No, do not be afraid of those nations, for the LORD your God is among you, and he is a great and awesome God."
>
> Deuteronomy 7:21 NLT

A powerful antidote to fear is awe of God. When you grasp that the God who is with you is the same God who created all things from nothing, fear is unmasked as a feeble enemy.

Of all of God's characteristics Moses could have focused on when delivering his charge to the Israelites, he chose the truth that God is *awesome*—beseeching Israel to remember that through all generations, God had brought people to their knees in wonder at His infinite power, unconditional love and intricate creation.

The relationship between awe of God and freedom from fear is profound. Awe is holy fear—an overwhelming awareness of God's power coupled with the knowledge that you are safe in His love. Earthly fear, however, is the enemy's false copy, a distorted version of awe where a sense of safety is replaced by one of danger.

If you have fallen for the enemy's distortion of awe, fearing created beings rather than marveling at the Creator, spend some time standing in awe of God. The more you reflect on who He is, the clearer it will become that He is far greater than all that you fear.

▶ **REFLECT** What aspects of God's character or creation bring me the most awe?

▶ **PRAY** Father God, You are awesome—Your power is vast, yet You care individually for each of Your children. You set the universe in motion, yet You know the number of hairs on my head. You created the mountains and the sea, yet You care about the troubles of my heart. Lead me into an increasing awe of who You are.

▶ **DECLARE** I serve a great and awesome God.

▶ **ACT** Go outside for five minutes and observe God's creation as though it is the first time you have seen it. Stand in awe at what He has made.

15 When You Are Outnumbered

"When you go out to battle against your enemies, and see horses and chariots and people more numerous than you, do not be afraid of them; for the LORD your God is with you, who brought you up from the land of Egypt."

Deuteronomy 20:1 NKJV

When the odds are against you, it may seem foolish *not* to fear. For the Christian, though, wisdom lies in exchanging fear for trust in God, because odds are nothing compared to His power.

The Israelites were commanded not to fear in a truly terrifying situation. By human predictions, going to battle while so outnumbered would mean certain death for thousands. The logical way to preserve their lives would be to stay where they were instead of advancing toward what God had promised. But it was those who tried to save their lives who forfeited the life God had for them—of the twelve spies who searched out the Promised Land, only Caleb and Joshua entered, because they trusted in God's promise of victory (see Numbers 14).

In the same way, God calls us to an illogical courage in situations we cannot overcome. It is difficult to reject fear when the odds are against us, but God is not bound by human mathematics. The God who proved the size of Israel's enemy irrelevant is the same God who is working *today* in the impossible situations we face.

With the God who can overcome even the worst of odds, you have no need to fear.

▶ **REFLECT** In what area of my life do I need to shift my gaze from the odds to the God who can overcome them?

▶ **PRAY** Father, the odds are against me in this trial I am facing, but You are not a God of human odds—You are the God of the improbable and the impossible. When I am outnumbered, help me to fix my eyes on You and trust that You will lead me to victory.

▶ **DECLARE** Numbers and odds are no match for God.

▶ **ACT** Ask a fellow believer to share a time when God overcame the odds in a trial he or she faced and call that story to mind the next time you feel outnumbered.

16 Spiritual Backing

> "He shall say to them, 'Hear, Israel, you are approaching the battle against your enemies today. Do not be fainthearted. Do not be afraid, or panic, or be terrified by them.'"
>
> Deuteronomy 20:3 NASB

Israel's victory did not depend upon the size or condition of their army, the number of their weaponry or the size of their cavalry. Israel's victory hinged only on whether the Lord was with them, and so does yours.

In Deuteronomy 20, the priest was commanded to lead the Israelite army into battle, and he encouraged them with the truth. This unconventional arrangement gives us insight into how differently we must approach battle compared to those engaged in conventional warfare.

The sights and sounds of an impending battle can be intimidating: the stomping foot; the loud, unfriendly shout; the angry face. But God says, "Hold on a minute. I need you to know just one thing: I am with you. So long as you are good with Me, you won't be facing this battle alone. Oh, and in case you're wondering, I've never lost a fight. Just keep calm, look the enemy in the eye and let Me fight for you!"

Backed by the encouragement of Jesus—your Great High Priest, who loves you and gave Himself for you in the battle for your soul—you can face your earthly battles with stouthearted courage.

▶ **REFLECT** In what situation do I need encouragement from God to take action?

▶ **PRAY** Father, may I face my battles today not in my own strength. Instead, may I trust in You and Your power to deliver me. Encourage me throughout my day with reminders of Your love, power and protection. Jesus, my Great High Priest, lead me into battle with Your wisdom and courage.

▶ **DECLARE** Every battle belongs to the Lord.

▶ **ACT** Encourage a friend who is struggling with fear with words that God has used to encourage you in your own battles.

God Goes with Me

"Be strong and courageous, do not be afraid or in dread of them, for the LORD your God is the One who is going with you. He will not desert you or abandon you."

Deuteronomy 31:6 NASB

The Scriptures reveal a God who never leaves His people's side. Whenever God called His people to face their fears, He went with them! Just as God went with His people, so will He go with *you*.

Moses knew that when it came time to take the Promised Land, the Israelites would be deathly afraid. Their fears would appear to be founded—when the twelve spies returned from scouting out the land, most would defeatedly report that compared to their enemies, they were "like grasshoppers" (Numbers 13:33 NASB). Anticipating the people's fear, Moses pointed them to the only part of the equation that mattered: The Lord was going with them. God was true to His word and led the people to victory through the power of His presence.

In the same way, God goes with *you*. In your daily rhythms, the Holy Spirit guides and comforts you. In difficult decisions, He gives you wisdom that goes beyond your own understanding. And when He calls you to act in audacious faith, He protects you from the enemy's attacks on your purpose in life.

You are never alone when you face your fears. As you go where God has called you to go, never forget that He is going *with* you.

▶ **REFLECT** How have I experienced God's presence at a time when I was afraid?

▶ **PRAY** Father, You are the God who goes with me, who gives me the gift of never being alone. You have never abandoned me, and You never will. As I face my fears, fill me with an awareness of Your presence, speak wisdom into my situation and show Your power where I am weak.

▶ **DECLARE** God goes with me wherever I go.

▶ **ACT** As you reflect on the truth that God goes with you, offer support to someone who is facing one of their fears, physically going with them, if possible.

18   God Goes before Me

"The LORD himself goes before you and will be with you;
he will never leave you nor forsake you. Do not be afraid;
do not be discouraged."

Deuteronomy 31:8 NIV

Many situations in life can make the future feel dark and uncertain. How can you take courage today when you do not know what tomorrow holds?

When we are lost and don't know the way forward, we all hope for the same thing: to meet someone *not* lost who is willing to lead us through the unfamiliar terrain and to our destination safely. We rely on this person's superior knowledge of the route as well as their benevolence toward us. We follow them because we trust they know the way to safety even if we do not.

What a comforting truth that our God already knows what awaits us in the future! He is not bound by space or time. Jesus sees the terrain ahead, difficult and smooth, and He Himself goes before us to lead us through. His wisdom and comfort will be with us whenever we feel lost or afraid.

No matter what the days ahead hold for you, do not be afraid or filled with dread. Keep your eyes on the one person whose Word is always true. Walk each day knowing you are safe because He who knows the path of your life—each and every moment—will be right there with you.

▶ **REFLECT** What uncertainties about the future can I trust to God's wisdom and love?

▶ **PRAY** Wise and loving Father, it comforts me to know that You always go ahead of me to lead me through whatever troubles I may face. My future may feel uncertain and frightening, but You will be with me. Thank You for promising Your presence to give me peace and courage every step of my way.

▶ **DECLARE** God goes before me.

▶ **ACT** Make a list of three ways in which God went before you that you see clearly now but couldn't see at the time.

19 A New Responsibility

"Have I not commanded you? Be strong and courageous. Do not be afraid; do not be discouraged, for the LORD your God will be with you wherever you go."

Joshua 1:9 NIV

Have you ever found yourself in a situation where you felt uncertain about your ability to perform your duties successfully?

Joshua had walked every step of the journey from Egypt to the edge of the Promised Land with Moses. Now, suddenly, Moses was no longer there, and God's people were all looking to him to lead the Hebrews into battle to take the land God had promised Abraham centuries earlier.

Joshua had the ability to choose faith over fear. God knew the potential was there for Joshua to be terrified by the magnitude of the responsibility, yet His commandment, which still reverberates today, is that both faith and fear are a choice.

There is an "aha" moment here that sometimes gets overlooked. The "aha" lies in the methodology God revealed to Joshua regarding how to trigger faith versus fear—constant meditation upon God, His promises and the memories of how He delivered the Hebrew nation from the beginning of the Egyptian plagues until that moment.

When God gives you a new responsibility, immediately go to His Word. As you meditate on the truth, your fears will fade and your courage will rise, readying you for the task to which God has called you.

▶ **REFLECT** What new responsibility do I need courage to fulfill?

▶ **PRAY** Father, I thank You for the strength to rise to any challenge to which You call me. As You commanded Joshua, help me to be strong and courageous so I, too, can prosper and have good success. I will look to Your Word, not my circumstances, to ensure I follow Your direction at every turn.

▶ **DECLARE** God's Word gives me courage.

▶ **ACT** Find three two-minute windows today to meditate on a favorite passage of Scripture that gives you strength or courage.

20 Do Not Be Discouraged

> Joshua said to them, "Do not be afraid; do not be discouraged. Be strong and courageous. This is what the LORD will do to all the enemies you are going to fight."
>
> Joshua 10:25 NIV

How are fear and discouragement connected? Discouragement can sap the power of one's faith as readily as fear can, but it is often more subtle in its approach.

Although God had given His immutable assurance that the Israelites would take the Promised Land from its inhabitants, forty years of wandering in the desert had left them discouraged. When it came time to take the land, discouragement had paved the path to immobilizing fear. When fear took root, the recent miracles God had done and His promises to defeat their enemies no longer rang true.

Speaking the very words God had spoken to him (see Joshua 1), Joshua exhorted the people not to be discouraged, but to be strong and courageous. They could shed the weight of their discouragement and fear and charge toward freedom because of who God was and what He had promised to do.

Only when the Israelites rejected discouragement were they able to lay hold of the courage that God offered them and enter the Promised Land.

If you live from an attitude of discouragement, you will never take hold of all God has for you. But if you fight discouragement with the truth of God's promises, He will strengthen you for the road ahead.

▶ **REFLECT** How did I remain courageous at a time when I could have become paralyzed by my fear?

▶ **PRAY** Father, thank You that You are my defense against any enemy that comes against me. Show me how to stand in faith despite the many times I am tempted to wither in fear. Teach me to discern the movement of the Holy Spirit so I can better respond to Your promptings as You guide me through seemingly risky circumstances.

▶ **DECLARE** God destroys my discouragement.

▶ **ACT** Make a list of every time God helped you overcome a threatening situation and review this list prior to facing a new situation that is producing uncertainty or fear.

21 God Gives the Victory

And the LORD said to Joshua, "Do not fear and do not be dismayed. Take all the fighting men with you, and arise, go up to Ai. See, I have given into your hand the king of Ai, and his people, his city, and his land."

Joshua 8:1 ESV

Have you ever felt defeated by fear before an adverse situation—paralyzed or unable to concentrate on anything?

If so, you are in good company. Joshua, the leader of Israel, and his elders were dismayed because they were unexpectedly defeated by their enemies. But once they sought the counsel of God, they understood the cause of their defeat and got rid of that obstacle as God commanded them. God then told Joshua to take all his men with him, arise and confront their enemy because He had given them into Joshua's hand.

God is the Giver of victory, and it brings honor to His great name to give us His victory. When we are surrounded by adversity, seeking the counsel of the Lord and staying attentive to His voice is essential. He gives us a strategy to follow, and once we implement it, He gives us the victory, His way.

Whatever you are facing, you do not need to fear because God will empower you with His divine strategy and plan. Fear not, nor dismay, for the Victor lives in you. Arise and go confront your adversity, knowing that He has already given you the victory.

▶ **REFLECT** What could be an obstacle to my victory?

▶ **PRAY** Father God, thank You for Your victory in advance. Lord, I need Your guidance today. Please give me a strategy to face the adversity and challenges of this day. I know You are the Victor who lives in me. Empower me to overcome any obstacles to gain the victory in my situation today.

▶ **DECLARE** God has given me the victory!

▶ **ACT** Make an inventory of all the past victories God has helped you to achieve.

22 Do Not Fear What They Fear

"Also I said to you, 'I am the LORD your God; do not fear the gods of the Amorites, in whose land you dwell.' But you have not obeyed My voice."

Judges 6:10 NKJV

Fear can be contagious. When those around you are afraid, your instincts may shout that you, too, should be afraid. As a child of the Most High God, though, you do not need to fear what others fear!

God's people had fallen into fear of the gods of those in their midst. Surrounded by people whose lives were consumed by the fear of idols, the memory of God's deliverance from Egypt grew dim. Rather than seek the Lord, they were swayed by popular opinion and sought powerless idols. It took the faith and courage of Gideon to snap Israel out of their fear and remind them of who God was (see Judges 6:11–7:25).

In the same way, we may forget God's past deliverance and latch on to the fears of those with whom we live, work or worship, assuming their alarmed reactions to personal circumstances or world events should also be our own.

The next time you sense yourself being pulled into the orbit of fear, remind yourself that God is your all-powerful Father and Protector. Stand your ground and hold on to the truth. Your courage will be a shining witness to God's glory and power in a world that is shackled by fear.

▶ **REFLECT** What am I fearing simply because those around me are afraid?

▶ **PRAY** Father God, You see the contagious fears that are common to the place I dwell, the anxiety and alarm that can infect me unless I remember who You are. Fill me anew with a deep revelation of Your love for me and Your power to save me from all my fears. All glory be to You, my Comforter and Protector.

▶ **DECLARE** God frees me from contagious fear.

▶ **ACT** Speak truth into a situation where fear has become contagious—if fear has spread among your family, church or friends, share a Scripture or testimony that points to God's power.

23 Approach God without Fear

> Now Gideon perceived that He was the Angel of the LORD. So Gideon said, "Alas, O Lord GOD! For I have seen the Angel of the LORD face to face."
>
> Then the LORD said to him, "Peace be with you; do not fear, you shall not die."
>
> Judges 6:22–23 NKJV

Do you have any reservations about drawing closer to God? Do you feel any fear when you think of boldly approaching His throne?

When a Visitor approached Gideon, spoke to him, accepted his sacrifice and then disappeared before his very eyes, Gideon was afraid and thought he would die because he had seen God's Angel. But the Lord spoke and assured him that he would not.

Throughout the Bible we see that all those who come humbly and sincerely to God seeking a closer relationship with Him are never rebuffed but rather are embraced and blessed by Him. The Lord will always encourage us to draw closer, just as He did with Gideon.

Because Christ has removed the barrier between God and anyone who accepts His work of salvation, you have nothing to fear. Today, draw nearer to Him and He will respond favorably. You don't need to hide your face in shame because you have been cleansed and forgiven.

As you stand boldly in His presence and gaze continuously upon the glory of the Lord, you will become transformed from glory to glory to become more like Him (2 Corinthians 3:18).

▶ **REFLECT** When did I last stand boldly in God's presence?

▶ **PRAY** Father, thank You that I do not need to be afraid of You. Your heart is never to harm or frighten me with Your power or holiness. Lord, as I approach You in reverent love and humility, draw closer to me that I may gaze upon You through the eyes of faith and be lifted out of my fear.

▶ **DECLARE** God invites me into His presence.

▶ **ACT** Set a time in your schedule to reread the Scripture for today and reflect on what it would be like to gaze upon the Lord face-to-face.

24

God Has Forgiven You

> "Don't be afraid," Samuel reassured them. "You have cer-
> tainly done wrong, but make sure now that you worship the
> Lord with all your heart, and don't turn your back on him."
>
> 1 Samuel 12:20 NLT

Have you ever committed a sin and then become fearful, thinking that God might not forgive you?

Sometimes we may feel afraid to approach God because of our sinful actions, especially as believers who "should have known better." The children of Israel were sinful, yet they were God's chosen people and God loved them. In 1 Samuel 12, the prophet Samuel encouraged the children of Israel to trust God and serve Him despite their sin.

God is ever mindful of our humanity, our propensity to sin and the fear we feel when we do. God has proven throughout eternity His love for us and the extent of His forgiveness. He wants us to embrace His forgiveness so much that He sent His Son, Jesus, to die on a rugged cross so that we wouldn't have to carry the weight of our sin.

It does not matter what you have done, how you have done it or whom you have done it with, God will forgive you. God is a good Father who loves you, and He tells you not to fear. He is an unchanging God, and just as He extended His forgiveness to the children of Israel, so He offers it to you.

▶ **REFLECT** In what area in my life have I feared that God would not forgive me?

▶ **PRAY** God, help me to release all fear at the foot of the cross. Lord, thank You for forgiving me for all my unrighteousness. Cleanse my ways, my heart and my thoughts. Help me to embrace Your forgiveness despite my sins. Teach me Your ways so that I won't keep falling into sin. Thank You, Lord.

▶ **DECLARE** God has already forgiven me.

▶ **ACT** As you ponder God's great forgiveness, forgive someone who has recently wronged you.

25

God Will Provide

"Do not fear; go and do as you have said, but make me a small cake from it first. . . . 'The bin of flour shall not be used up, nor shall the jar of oil run dry, until the day the LORD sends rain.'"

1 Kings 17:13–14 NKJV

Fear of not being provided for or not having enough to make ends meet is an almost-universal human experience. When God is present in your life, though, so are miracles, including those of miraculous provision.

The account of the widow of Zarephath reveals how God provides in times of need. God sent a severe drought upon Israel as punishment for wickedness. After several years, the Lord told Elijah to travel past the northern border of Israel to Sidon, where He had commanded a widow to take care of him. When Elijah arrived, the widow appeared not to expect his arrival. But Elijah spoke what God had told him, and the widow believed this strange prophet whom she had only just met!

Miracles began for her when she acted on the word of the Lord, and so will they for you. He has promised never to leave you or give up on you. He has counseled you to ask Him for daily provision. And He would not tell you to ask for what He would not provide.

You do not need to fear that you will not have enough. God has promised to provide for your needs, and He is always true to His Word.

▶ **REFLECT** How has God provided for my physical needs in the past?

▶ **PRAY** Father, I praise You for telling me to bring my daily needs to You so that You can supply them. Thank You for all You have already so faithfully and wonderfully provided for me. Cause my heart to rest confidently in You and never fret over what I need. In Jesus' name, I pray, Amen.

▶ **DECLARE** God supplies my daily needs.

▶ **ACT** Ask God to place someone on your heart, and let Him use you to provide for one of their daily needs, whether it is material, financial or spiritual.

26 God's Constant Affirmation

> The angel of the LORD said to Elijah, "Go down with him;
> do not be afraid of him." So Elijah got up and went down
> with him to the king.
>
> 2 Kings 1:15 NIV

Wouldn't it be great to have God's assurance that a given situation was going to conclude in your favor?

How devoid of fear would you be if the Lord's angel showed up and told you, "Hey, everything is going to be all right with that current crisis you are facing"? Would that be the end of every negative emotion?

It is interesting to note that despite having called down fire on two separate occasions, resulting in the deaths of over one hundred enemy soldiers, Elijah still needed God's angel to assure him not to fear in the new situation in which he found himself.

Just like Elijah, when we are facing a new and scary situation, the present threat often seems much more real than God's past deliverance. Although we are benefactors of even better promises than the ones Elijah benefited from (see Hebrews 8:6), we also need God's revealed Word to keep us free from fear.

God has compassion upon your tendency to fear and lavishes reminders of His love and protection in each new situation. When you are afraid, look to Him, and He will assure you again and again that He is with you.

▶ **REFLECT** How has God reminded me not to fear?

▶ **PRAY** Father God, lead me away from the stressful pathways that surround me in daily life into green pastures of peace. Your Word is a lamp unto my feet and a light unto my path. Remind me that though the destination may currently be unclear, You are always with me and will never forsake me.

▶ **DECLARE** God reminds me not to fear.

▶ **ACT** As you ponder God's repeated affirmation of His love for you, give verbal affirmation to someone in your life, reminding him or her of your love.

27

Seeing with Spiritual Eyes

"Don't be afraid," the prophet answered. "Those who are with us are more than those who are with them." And Elisha prayed, "Open his eyes, LORD, so that he may see." Then the LORD opened the servant's eyes, and he looked and saw the hills full of horses and chariots of fire all around Elisha.

2 Kings 6:16–17 NIV

In the trials you are facing, you may *appear* outnumbered and unprotected, but nothing could be further from the truth. Looking through spiritual eyes, you will see that God is surrounding you with abundant protection.

When the king of Syria surrounded the prophet Elisha with bloodthirsty troops, Elisha remained strangely calm. He saw something that his fearful servant couldn't see through natural eyes—that forces more powerful than all of Syria were protecting them.

Like Elisha's servant, we often view our trials through a material lens, forgetting the spiritual reality that undergirds every aspect of the Christian life. As the apostle Paul reminds us, "Our struggle is not against flesh and blood, but . . . against the powers of this dark world and against the spiritual forces of evil in the heavenly realms" (Ephesians 6:12 NIV). And as believers, we know who ultimately wins this epic battle—our Lord Jesus Christ!

When what you see provokes you to fear, ask the Holy Spirit to open your spiritual eyes. He will be faithful to show you that you are protected, you are loved and you have no need to fear.

▶ **REFLECT** In what situations has God protected me when I appeared to be outnumbered?

▶ **PRAY** Father, You are my great Protector. I praise You for Your protection in the past and in the present. Open my spiritual eyes to the reality of Your protection as I step out in courage this week. When I appear to be outnumbered, remind me of the account of Elisha and tether me to the truth of Your Word.

▶ **DECLARE** God opens my eyes to the truth.

▶ **ACT** Ask God to help you make a list of the ways He has protected you in the past—at times when you might have not recognized it was Him. Remind yourself to look at situations from God's victorious point of view.

28

Reject the Enemy's Lies

> And Isaiah said to them, "This is what you shall say to your master: 'The LORD says this: "Do not be fearful because of the words that you have heard, with which the servants of the king of Assyria have blasphemed Me."'"
>
> 2 Kings 19:6 NASB

All around, you see conflict and a continuation of long-standing troubles. The enemy tells you, "It's over." What can you do when the enemy's words seem truer than God's promises?

Hezekiah, king of Judah, shows us how to reject the enemy's lies. Sennacherib, king over the Assyrian empire, was on an expansionary drive. Among other conquests, he had recently added the northern kingdom of Israel to his huge empire. Now he sent a delegation to Jerusalem telling Hezekiah to surrender immediately or else! To ramp up pressure, the delegation met outside the city gate and made their boasts and threats public before the men on the wall.

Most kings would throw in the towel at this point, but not Hezekiah. Hezekiah humbly took his problem to the Lord in prayer and then sent for the prophet to inquire of God.

How wonderful that we can take our troubles to the Lord. Rather than being intimidated by threats and lies, we can receive assurance and help from Him.

As you turn to the Lord, the enemy will turn away from you. Like Hezekiah, as you pray and trust, you will see the salvation of your God.

▶ **REFLECT** How and about what has the enemy been lying to me?

▶ **PRAY** Father, thank You that every cycle of doubt or fear the enemy has sought to bring into my life is broken, because I decide to follow You wholeheartedly and trust only in You. Today I bring each doubt and fear before Your throne. Repel the lies of the enemy and confirm the truth of Your grace and power!

▶ **DECLARE** God destroys the enemy's lies.

▶ **ACT** Speak truth to a friend or family member whom the enemy is trying to convince that "it's over."

29

Emboldened by Obedience

> "Then you will prosper, if you take care to fulfill the statutes and judgments with which the LORD charged Moses concerning Israel. Be strong and of good courage; do not fear nor be dismayed."
>
> 1 Chronicles 22:13 NKJV

When a task seems too great, your first instinct may be to fear failure. Obedience is a powerful weapon against fear. When you focus on pleasing God rather than achieving an outcome, the fear of failure loses its power.

King Solomon was tasked with the immense responsibility of building the Lord's temple. Given the sacredness of the task, King David knew that his son would be vulnerable to the fear of failure. David's wise words to Solomon speak to us today: If we approach our tasks with a heart focused on pleasing the Lord, God will prosper us in *His* way. In God's eyes, true success lies not in a "perfect" outcome resulting from human resources, but in understanding and knowing Him (see Jeremiah 9:23–24).

When we fear an unfavorable outcome, we are often timid in our actions even though we have the freedom in

Christ to take bold steps of faith. If we shift our eyes from the outcome to the love and grace of the One who has called us, we can obey without fearing failure.

When you are committed to obeying God, you have no need to fear the outcome. As you take audacious steps of faith, He will bless your obedience.

▶ **REFLECT** In what area do I fear failure and instead need to step out in obedience to God?

▶ **PRAY** Gracious Father, the fear of failure has tempted me to be timid, but You have not given me a spirit of fear, but of power, love and a sound mind. I want to obey You in the tasks You have given me and to trust You with the outcome. As I step out in faith, prosper me in Your way and in Your timing.

▶ **DECLARE** Obeying God brings freedom.

▶ **ACT** Take a step of bold obedience to God in an area in which you have been afraid to act.

30 Do Not Fear Failure

> David also said to Solomon his son, "Be strong and coura-
> geous, and do the work. Do not be afraid or discouraged,
> for the LORD God, my God, is with you. He will not fail you or
> forsake you until all the work for the service of the temple
> of the LORD is finished."
>
> 1 Chronicles 28:20 NIV

Have you ever resisted doing what God had called you to
do because you were afraid of failing?

When Solomon was given the immense task of building
the temple, he likely feared failure as well. Realizing that
his son would be overwhelmed by such a weighty responsibility, King David encouraged Solomon from a place of
wisdom and experience. During his lifetime, David encoun-
tered plenty of opportunities to trust God, from needing
His protection while on the run from King Saul to replacing
fear with faith in both battle and leadership.

King David confidently counseled Solomon, assuring him
that God could be trusted and that as Solomon pursued
God's instruction, he did not need to fear failure. Solomon
was empowered to pursue the work of God without fear,
confident that God would help him build the temple.

In our lives, too, God will ensure that His work gets done. God never said we would not fail. But He promised us He would not leave us, and He promised that He would cause us to triumph in *His* way.

Just as Solomon found solace in the words of his father, David, your Father in heaven will see to it that you can accomplish His will without fearing failure.

▶ **REFLECT** In what area(s) in my life am I afraid to fail and why?

▶ **PRAY** God, help me to trust You in every area of my life. Lord, help me surrender my fears to You, especially the fear of failure. When I fail, remind me that You are there to pick me up and help me start again. Help me see failure as an opportunity to grow in grace, maturity and humility.

▶ **DECLARE** God frees me from the fear of failure.

▶ **ACT** Take one step toward a goal that you have been avoiding out of fear of failure.

31   God Is Fighting for You

"This is what the LORD says: Do not be afraid! Don't be discouraged by this mighty army, for the battle is not yours, but God's."

2 Chronicles 20:15 NLT

It is natural to feel afraid or powerless upon receiving some unexpected news about your health, finances, career or an important relationship. The question is how you will approach that challenging moment.

Difficult times like these are inevitable, but they can take us into a deeper understanding of the power of the God we serve and His love for us. Imagine being King Jehoshaphat and receiving the dismaying news that a mighty army has declared war against you and your people. Jehoshaphat felt terrified and powerless when he received this news, but he cried out to God, seeking His guidance. Encouraged by the prophet Jahaziel's proclamation that "the battle was not [his], but God's," the king went boldly into battle, and God gave him the victory.

Just as King Jehoshaphat did, when we feel powerless, we need to depend on the power of the almighty God, the only One who has the power to fight and win our battles.

Life is filled with many challenging moments and difficult seasons, but there is good news. You do not need to worry or be dismayed, because even though you might not see it yet, the battle is already won!

▶ **REFLECT** How did I approach the last time I felt terrified or powerless upon receiving some unexpected news?

▶ **PRAY** Father God, thank You for reminding me that You are the One who fights my battles when I feel powerless. Lord, help me depend on You with confidence as I seek Your guidance through these times, and give me new revelation and understanding of Your power and love. I know You are fighting every battle for me.

▶ **DECLARE** My battle is already won!

▶ **ACT** Pray with a friend or family member over a battle you are facing.

God's Unlimited Power

"Be strong and courageous. Do not be afraid or dismayed before the king of Assyria and all the horde that is with him, for there are more with us than with him. With him is an arm of flesh, but with us is the LORD our God, to help us and to fight our battles." And the people took confidence from the words of Hezekiah king of Judah.

2 Chronicles 32:7–8 ESV

In a world that is increasingly hostile to Christians, it is easy to fear what people may do if you stand up for the truth. Remember, though, that God limits human power, while God's power is *unlimited*!

God's people were in a terrifying situation—King Sennacherib, one of the most powerful rulers in the world, was threatening them with war. The faithful King Hezekiah refused to fear, though; instead, he proclaimed that Sennacherib was powerless compared to the Lord. Sennacherib had "an arm of flesh," meaning he was only a weak, vulnerable human. No matter how powerful he seemed, he had limited time on earth, determined by the God whose people he was attempting to conquer.

Hezekiah's words speak to us today. Whoever threatens us has only "an arm of flesh," whereas we have the eternally powerful God with us. When the fear of people tempts us to compromise, may we remember that man's days are "like grass. . . . But from everlasting to everlasting the LORD's love is with those who fear him" (Psalm 103:15, 17 NIV).

You serve the God of eternal, unlimited power who wants to help you fight your battles. Stand firm in your faith and watch Him act on your behalf.

▶ **REFLECT** In what area have I been tempted to compromise out of fear of what others may do to me?

▶ **PRAY** Father God, I confess that fear of what people may do to me has influenced my actions. When people tempt me to dishonor Your name, help me to stand firm in the authority I have in Christ and the confidence I have in Your eternal power. Give me courage and an unwavering heart, that I may bring glory to Your name.

▶ **DECLARE** God empowers me to stand up for truth.

▶ **ACT** In a situation where you are tempted to compromise, make a "game plan" with another believer of how you will respond, and ask that person to keep you accountable.

33 | Confronting Fear Courageously

> "When I saw their fear, I stood and said to the nobles, the officials, and the rest of the people: 'Do not be afraid of them; remember the Lord who is great and awesome, and fight for your brothers, your sons, your daughters, your wives, and your houses.'"
>
> Nehemiah 4:14 NASB

What emotions do you feel when you hear the word *confrontation*? For many, the thought of confrontation evokes a sense of dread. Confrontation can be scary, but sometimes it is how God calls you to fight!

When God charged Nehemiah to rebuild the wall of Jerusalem, he faced intense opposition, especially from an official named Sanballat and his followers. Most things God commands us to do are not without obstacles, but it is in facing those obstacles in faith that we see God's power.

Winning the battle against fear is only done by looking fear in the face and recognizing that with God, you are a threat to the spirit of fear. Nehemiah recognized that the only way to defeat Sanballat was to confront him. When insulted by Sanballat and others angry that the Jews were rebuilding the wall, Nehemiah did not retreat, but he charged his people to keep on building, trusting that God would empower them to finish the task to which He had called them.

We must also courageously confront fear through faith and hope in God, then pursue that which fear told us not to do.

As you confront your fears, remember the courage of Nehemiah and stand firm. God will bless your courage and trust in Him.

▶ **REFLECT** What do I need courage to confront today?

▶ **PRAY** God, I know that fear does not come from You and that it has no power over me. Help me to confront my fears today, trusting in Your support and protection. Father, give me the courage to fight for all that You have given me. Keep me grounded in Your character and in Your Word.

▶ **DECLARE** God helps me confront my fears.

▶ **ACT** Confront one of your fears today, whether it means bringing up a difficult conversation, stepping out of your comfort zone or saying no to something.

Your Loving Shepherd

> Even though I walk through the valley of the shadow of death, I will fear no evil, for you are with me; your rod and your staff, they comfort me.
>
> Psalm 23:4 ESV

The longer you live, the more you are likely to walk through times of grief. The psalmist David, in this much-loved psalm, tells you how.

David, who had faced a giant, fought many battles, witnessed many deaths and fled for his life to caves in the wilderness, knew a lot about grief. He had felt the personal loss of transitioning from national champion and hero to becoming the most wanted and hunted enemy of the king. Yet somehow, David continued to act with courage and hope in God. How did he do this?

First, David kept walking. When life is hard, it is wise to avoid going to the side of the road and sitting down. You won't progress. Second, David refused to fear evil because God was with him. David did not blame the Lord for his troubles. On the contrary, David was comforted in his troubles because God was with him as a Shepherd with His sheep.

Even in the darkest places, the Lord is with you. In His hand are His rod to protect you from enemies and His staff to guide you in the best way. He will lead you through the valley and out to the other side.

▶ **REFLECT** In what ways has the Lord been a shepherd to me recently?

▶ **PRAY** Father, when my life leads me onto a dark path, help me to keep on walking. May I know that You are with me and that I can rejoice in Your presence. I praise You for protecting me from every unseen enemy of doubt, fear and evil and for guiding me to a brighter path.

▶ **DECLARE** My loving Shepherd leads me.

▶ **ACT** As David kept walking through the valley of the shadow of death, do something today that will help you to keep moving forward in your most difficult trial.

35 The Lord Is My Light

> The LORD is my light and my salvation; whom shall I fear?
> The LORD is the stronghold of my life; of whom shall I be
> afraid?
>
> Psalm 27:1 ESV

This fallen world is dark—you don't have to look far to see the pain and evil birthed by sin. With God, though, you don't need to fear the darkness, for He is your Light!

Five hundred years before Jesus' birth, Isaiah proclaimed the coming Savior by saying that "the people walking in darkness have seen a great light" (Isaiah 9:2 NIV). This is both a solid reality and a beautiful metaphor. The darkness of sin clouds our vision, intensifies fear and imprisons us, but Jesus, our Light, reveals things as they are and sets us free from sin and fear.

When the world's darkness beckons us to fear, His Light lets us see further than the darkness allows—we can see that our pain is temporary, we have the hope of eternity and He is coming soon. When we choose the darkness of sin, the Light reveals our faults and lovingly calls us to repentance. As John wrote, the darkness cannot overcome the Light (see John 1:5), no matter how hard it tries.

The Light of the World is with you to illuminate your present path and reveal your future hope. With the incarnate Light by your side, you need not fear the darkness.

▶ **REFLECT** What area of my life do I need God to flood with His Light?

▶ **PRAY** Jesus, You are the Light who illuminates my darkness. I praise You for coming to this dark world in human flesh for my sake—that Your love for me is so deep that You gave Your life to deliver me from darkness. Empower me to walk in Your light all the days of my life.

▶ **DECLARE** The Lord is my Light.

▶ **ACT** Light a candle and meditate on the truth that Jesus is the Light.

36 When You Are Attacked

> Though a mighty army surrounds me, my heart will not be afraid. Even if I am attacked, I will remain confident.
>
> Psalm 27:3 NLT

As a boy, he killed a lion, a bear and a giant. As a warrior, he fought thousands. As a king, he founded a dynasty and united scattered tribes. What was the secret to this man's courage and success?

King David's two statements in Psalm 27 capture the reason he could continuously face danger and overcome the odds against him. He did not trust in his own abilities. He did not let his circumstances affect his confidence. He relied entirely on one person: The Lord was his light, his strength and his salvation.

David references enemies of war as a source of fear. While we may never find ourselves in that exact circumstance, we certainly experience the sense of being surrounded or attacked by destructive forces. In our fallen world, it is easy to see the potential for harm in many different forms and to feel threatened by many types of danger.

Just as David did, we have a choice: to respond with fear and discouragement or to trust in the Lord.

Let your heart be encouraged by David's testimony. Time after time, God delivered him both from evil and from the fear of it. He can do the same for you.

▶ **REFLECT** In what area do I feel attacked and in need of God's assistance?

▶ **PRAY** Lord, thank You for David's experience. He trusted You, and You delivered him from harm. When I feel surrounded by threats or am fearful of attack, help me respond with faith. You have so much more power than my enemies. Your promises are true in every circumstance. Let my heart be confident in Your light, strength and salvation.

▶ **DECLARE** God prevails over my attackers.

▶ **ACT** Listen to a worship song that reminds you of God's power in your battles. Meditate on the lyrics and ask God to strengthen your heart against fear.

37 Seek God First

I sought the LORD, and he answered me and delivered me from all my fears.

Psalm 34:4 ESV

When your fears threaten to overwhelm you, where do you turn first to find relief? Jesus wants you to seek Him first whenever you feel afraid.

King David, the author of Psalm 34, feared for his life multiple times at every stage of his life—as a boy, young man, young adult and king. But he learned early in life to seek first after God, who was "a very present help in trouble" (Psalm 46:1 ESV).

To seek God means to turn to Him, to rely on His character and strength. But how do we do that when there are so many other things to turn to instead—options that may give temporary relief but only disappoint us in the end?

We seek God first by humbly and repeatedly asking Him for His help as often as we feel afraid. We seek God through worship, individually and corporately, proclaiming His worth and our reliance on His care. And we seek God through studying His Word, on our own and with other believers in whom the Holy Spirit abides.

The next time anxiety burdens your heart, earnestly seek the Lord first. He will answer and deliver you from all your fears!

▶ **REFLECT** Where do I turn first for help when I feel afraid?

▶ **PRAY** Faithful Father, You are the one person on whom I can completely rely. Whenever I turn to You, You are with me. You see all my cares and are bigger than my problems. You answer me with help that sets me free from my fears. Please help me seek You first whenever I feel anxious or afraid.

▶ **DECLARE** Seeking God first frees me from fear.

▶ **ACT** Block off ten minutes in your day to give your burdens to God or to sing songs of worship. Do it at the start of your day or *before* an activity that typically causes stress or anxiety.

Even the Wind and Waves

God is our refuge and strength, a very present help in trouble. Therefore we will not fear though the earth gives way, though the mountains be moved into the heart of the sea, though its waters roar and foam, though the mountains tremble at its swelling.

Psalm 46:1–3 ESV

Lack of control over difficult circumstances can be fertile ground for fear to grow. If anxiety sprouts over the uncontrollable, remember that you serve the God who is in control of all things.

The psalmist's description of the mountains crashing into the sea is a vivid picture of circumstances beyond our control. The earth may not literally give way, but a cancer diagnosis, a relational rift or a long-unanswered prayer may make us feel as though our world is crumbling. It is in these times that Jesus wants to refine our faith.

About nine hundred years after the psalm was written, Jesus' disciples found themselves living out Psalm 46: They were caught in a raging storm that threatened them with death. Jesus calmed the storm, and in awe they marveled that "even the winds and the waves obey him" (Matthew 8:27 NIV). Two thousand years later, we serve the same God and have the same opportunity to trust.

You serve the God who has calmed deadly storms with just a word, the God whom you can trust completely with your heart and with your future. In the fertile ground of uncontrollable circumstances, let faith grow instead of fear.

▶ **REFLECT** In what situation do I need to run to God as my refuge?

▶ **PRAY** Holy Father, when it feels like everything around me is crumbling, may I remember that You are in control and are holding me close. No matter what comes today, this week or this year, You are my ever-present refuge and strength. Thank You for Your comfort, love and protection over my life.

▶ **DECLARE** God is my refuge and strength.

▶ **ACT** Spend a few minutes in nature and meditate on the fact that everything you see was created by God and is subject to Him.

39   When the Days Are Evil

> Why should I fear in the days of evil, when the iniquity at my heels surrounds me? Those who trust in their wealth and boast in the multitude of their riches, none of them can by any means redeem his brother, nor give to God a ransom for him.
>
> Psalm 49:5–7 NKJV

Does the evil of the world strike fear into your heart? When violence and perversion surround you, remember that the days of evil are numbered. Soon, Jesus will return and destroy evil for all eternity.

Sin has always permeated our fallen world, but in our globalized age, we not only experience evil in our daily lives, but are overwhelmed by images of war, abuse and slavery from around the world. We not only see evil forces striving to silence the Gospel where we live, but we hear reports of our brothers and sisters being killed because of their faith. Evil people near and far boastfully perpetuate the enemy's schemes, acting as though they are immortal. As King David said, they seem to "have no struggles; their bodies are healthy and strong" (Psalm 73:4 NIV).

Psalm 49 reminds us that evil may threaten, but God's goodness has the last word. The enemy's time is short, and his power is limited. God has already written the final chapter of Jesus' triumphant return and the destruction of all evil. While you wait for these things to take place, take comfort in the truth that His goodness will soon conquer all evil.

▶ **REFLECT** In what situation can I exercise faith in God's goodness rather than the fear of human evil?

▶ **PRAY** Lord God, when the evil in the world feels overwhelming, strengthen my mind with the truth that Your goodness will ultimately wipe out all evil and restore the world when Jesus returns. As I wait for Your return, arm me with the sword of Your Word, that I may fight confidently against the darkness of the present world.

▶ **DECLARE** God's goodness conquers evil.

▶ **ACT** Today, avoid all media that sparks fear of evil, and do something that reminds you of God's goodness, such as talking with a friend, baking something delicious or spending time in nature.

40 Trust in God's Word

> When I am afraid, I put my trust in you. In God, whose word I praise, in God I trust; I shall not be afraid. What can flesh do to me?
>
> Psalm 56:3–4 ESV

The word *trust* in these two verses comes from an old Semitic root word meaning to "lie down on the ground."

Historically, when some in the Middle East carried deadly swords, the action of lying down before another person demonstrated complete trust in the person not to kill them, but to protect them from nearby danger.

David was saying to God, "I trust You completely. I disarm myself before You. I know You will not harm me. I know in Your presence I am fully protected from harm." That's how David dealt with fear. He had a whole army looking for him, but he was able to lie down before God and relax! He was persuaded that God was stronger than anything men could do to him. What led David to this courageous trust?

David had learned to wrest his attention away from what evil men were doing and to fix his gaze upon God's Word, His past kindnesses and His sure promises. When fears came, this holy focus enabled David to stand firm.

If you are afraid of what's in front of you, lift your gaze to your Creator, and His words will renew your courage, reminding you that you can fully trust Him.

▶ **REFLECT** How can I fix my gaze upon God today?

▶ **PRAY** Father, I thank You that in Your presence I can disarm myself. I don't need to defend myself from You. I praise You that I am fully protected in Your presence. I rejoice in Your kindnesses toward me and Your promises. Help me to fulfill my promises toward You and not to fear any human or what they might do to me.

▶ **DECLARE** God can always be trusted.

▶ **ACT** Take a moment to lie down in the presence of God and relax, sing a song of praise or worship and think of His kindnesses and His promises to you.

41

Under God's Wings

> He will cover you with his pinions, and under his wings
> you will find refuge; his faithfulness is a shield and buckler.
> You will not fear the terror of the night, nor the arrow
> that flies by day.
>
> Psalm 91:4–5 ESV

People around the world treasure Psalm 91 because it speaks peace and comfort into the storms and fears of life. It speaks of God Most High as being the ultimate refuge, the One who is most highly exalted, yet intimate.

God is depicted in this psalm as a bird spreading His mighty wings over the one seeking His refuge. The "refugee" is covered by the entire strength of the wing structure that provides protection from the environment. Many scholars recognize this psalm as being not only full of similes, but also being filled with spiritual metaphors that illustrate how God defends us from evil and spiritual attack. He does this by putting us under His direct protection and comforting us as a mother bird protects her young under her wings.

Of course, we are not taken hostage by God; we must go to that place willingly. Jesus lamented of His longing to protect Jerusalem like a hen protecting her chicks, but its inhabitants were not willing (see Luke 13:34).

Today, willingly come under God's tender covering. You will be embraced by His warm, intimate presence, which comforts and protects.

▶ **REFLECT** How has God shielded me under the shadow of His wings?

▶ **PRAY** Father, help me learn to dwell in that secret place where You are, where no enemy can enter, harm or disturb me. Rather than fight my own battles, I choose to humble myself and come under Your shelter, where I shall be safe and greatly comforted. Thank You for the loving protection of Your wings.

▶ **DECLARE** God protects me under His wings.

▶ **ACT** Spend some time today in a place where you feel especially safe (a room in your house, somewhere in nature, etc.) and reflect on the loving protection of God's wings.

42

Comfort in Anxiety

> In the multitude of my anxieties within me, Your comforts delight my soul.
>
> Psalm 94:19 NKJV

Anxiety is not new. It is a state of distress or uneasiness that can affect all people. The Bible gives honest accounts of believers struggling mentally, and it describes minds and emotions flooded with stress, hyperactive to threats and unable to reason.

In this verse, the psalmist admits anxiety issues. Previously in the psalm, he expresses dismay at the evil men and injustices around him and uncertainty about his own well-being and future. He is overwhelmed from within.

Anxious thoughts tend to multiply, disrupting our focus and even our ability to function. Indeed, there are times when our inner world contains as much darkness and distress as the outer world. This is our fallen reality. Is there any remedy?

Earthly comforts can alleviate our anxieties to an extent. But God's comforts—His Word and His Spirit—minister on a soul level, addressing our fears at the root. And He does not wait until we are in a better frame of mind to offer

Himself. In a "multitude of anxieties," God opens His arms, ready to comfort us.

Any given day may bring anxiety, but God is always there to comfort you. Trust Him to meet you, inner chaos and all, and soothe your inner soul in the deepest way.

▶ **REFLECT** How do I tend to deal with my anxiety?

▶ **PRAY** God, I have anxieties within me. Sometimes fearful thoughts completely overwhelm me. Thank You for meeting me and ministering to me in those moments. You are able to bring order to my mind, calm to my emotions and better yet, joy to my soul. When I am anxious, help me to receive Your comforts.

▶ **DECLARE** God comforts me when I am anxious.

▶ **ACT** Write down a list of your current anxieties, then give them to God and crumple up the paper. Ask for His comfort and expect the Holy Spirit to move on your behalf.

43 Defiant Courage

The LORD is on my side; I will not fear. What can man do
to me?

Psalm 118:6 ESV

Have you ever been bullied or made to feel ashamed and
afraid? With God on your side, you can have defiant courage
in the face of your enemy's intimidation or threats.

Most of the conflicts we experience in life can be handled
through reasonable means. But sometimes we face people
who intimidate or bully us to get their own way. They may
threaten us directly or use subtle ways to manipulate our
emotions and cause confusion and fear. Even our culture
can make us feel like we are doing something wrong and
pressure us into conformity and silence. And behind it all
stands our accuser, the devil, spreading his condemning lies
to make God's children feel powerless and afraid.

But we can take courage! The God of the universe—the
Author of all life and Ruler over every principality—is on
our side! Nothing can truly hurt us because His authority
trumps any evil intention against us. By dying on the cross
and living again, Jesus defied His accusers by showing that
His Father was on His side.

As His follower, you can stand unafraid, knowing the Lord is on your side, no matter who stands against you.

▶ **REFLECT** In what current situation can I have defiant courage against bullying and intimidation, knowing that God is with me?

▶ **PRAY** Lord Jesus, help me be courageous when people try to intimidate me or threaten harm. Give me wisdom as to how to exercise courage in my situation; I know it may not mean fighting back. Help me to stand unafraid, knowing You are on my side. Free me from the fear of man as I seek to please You first.

▶ **DECLARE** The Lord gives me courage to face every adversary.

▶ **ACT** In an area where you have been intimidated, take a defiant step of faith: Speak up for yourself, replace a fearful thought with truth or leave a harmful situation.

44 Rest in Crisis

> You will not be subject to terror, for it will not terrify you. Nor will the disrespectful be able to push you aside, because God is your confidence in times of crisis, keeping your heart at rest in every situation.
>
> Proverbs 3:25–26 TPT

Has an unexpected crisis, the passing of a loved one, a job loss or a negative medical report filled you with fear?

You are not alone. Most of us have experienced times when unexpected crises have made us feel fearful and powerless. Satan is notorious for inciting fear in our lives. He is masterful at the power of suggestion and uses fear to torment and terrorize us. Yet in even the scariest of situations, God is completely trustworthy. Circumstances can bully us emotionally, but God's Word is more powerful than our emotions. We can use the truth in God's Word to help combat fear in our lives and keep our hearts at rest.

Second Timothy 1:7 says, "God has not given us a spirit of fear, but of power and of love and of a sound mind" (NKJV). Proverbs 3:25–26 reminds us that God is our confidence, and He will give us a restful spirit when crises beg for our hearts to panic and collapse.

God is the Master of your crises, and fear has no power over you. As you put your confidence in God, you can boldly declare to all fear-provoking circumstances, "I am not afraid!"

▶ **REFLECT** What crisis or devastating news do I need God's courage to face?

▶ **PRAY** Heavenly Father, thank You that You have given me power, love and a sound mind. Thank You for the power to overcome fear. Thank You for rest in the midst of scary situations. Thank You for not letting terror terrify me. Thank You for being my confidence in times of crisis.

▶ **DECLARE** God puts my heart at rest.

▶ **ACT** As you reflect on God's gift of a restful heart, take at least ten minutes today doing something you find restful.

45

Seeing from God's Perspective

"And say to him, 'Be careful, be quiet, do not fear, and do not let your heart be faint because of these two smoldering stumps of firebrands, at the fierce anger of Rezin and Syria and the son of Remaliah.'"

Isaiah 7:4 ESV

Do you have a fear so big that it spills into every area of your life, constantly disrupting your thoughts and affecting your actions? A key to fighting this fear is praying to see it through God's eyes.

In this Old Testament passage, King Ahaz and the people of Judah were deeply affected by a report that suggested war and potential death were imminent. Yet God, through His prophet Isaiah, disregards their fear and instead speaks with absolute disdain about the impending threat.

From God's perspective, these two imminent threats were already extinguished, smoldering remains of a once-burning flame. God, through Isaiah, clearly said they were not worthy of the fear King Ahaz and the people of Judah were experiencing in response to their threats.

The things you fear the most, too, are "smoldering stumps of firebrands" in God's eyes. What strikes fear into your heart does not scare Him at all. The next time something seems big enough to do you harm, remember that God probably has a different point of view. Take a moment in prayer to get His perspective because God is always bigger than your biggest fear.

► **REFLECT** In what area might my level of fear decrease if I saw the situation from God's perspective?

► **PRAY** Father, help me to develop Your perspective in all I do. May I not react to evil reports, but instead get quiet so I can receive and believe the "report of the Lord." Bring me closer to You through the presence of Your Holy Spirit so that my feet are anchored by the truth You reveal to me on a moment-by-moment basis.

► **DECLARE** God's perspective frees me from fear.

► **ACT** Ask two friends to share about a time when God overcame a fear in their lives that seemed too big for them.

46

They Fear, We Trust

> Don't believe their every conspiracy rumor. And don't fear
> what they fear—don't be moved or terrified.
>
> Isaiah 8:12 TPT

Fear can grip your heart at any given moment, especially when everyone else is terrified.

Isaiah 8:12 is a reminder of how followers of Jesus should respond to what terrifies the world. God wants us to be an example of trust in the midst of terrifying circumstances and to demonstrate where our faith lies at all times. The world is groaning and searching for consistent peace from the terror of the turbulent times in which we live. We hinder the movement of God in the lives of others who are watching us when we are moved like the world. It is foolishness to assume we won't face scary things, but we must respond in trust and not fear.

Our ability to trust God instead of succumbing to fear grows as we experience fearful circumstances, terrifying crises and alarming occurrences. The more they happen, the more we can shift our faith into action, and the more we will walk in trust. Because we trust God and have experienced

His love countless times, fear's tormenting power is eradicated in our lives.

God needs His children to show the world that He can be trusted in everything. Will you show the world that God can be trusted by your response to fear?

▶ **REFLECT** When have I been a beacon of light during a scary situation?

▶ **PRAY** Father, I am grateful that I don't have to be afraid of the terrors by night or the arrows by day. God, thank You for reminding me that I should not walk by what I see, but by faith. Thank You for calming every raging sea in my life. You are my peace in the midst of chaos. Amen.

▶ **DECLARE** Jesus has overcome the world.

▶ **ACT** Ask a friend or family member about their fears. Pray for him or her.

47

Assurance of Your Salvation

> "Surely God is my salvation; I will trust and not be afraid. The LORD, the LORD himself, is my strength and my defense; he has become my salvation."
>
> Isaiah 12:2 NIV

As a believer in Jesus, you can be 100 percent sure of your salvation. In a world where little is certain, you can know that you are eternally His, and you never need to fear that He will leave you.

Imagine yourself standing at the base of the world's largest mountain, Mount Everest, which stands 29,032 feet above sea level. Imagine God the Father Himself placing you on His shoulders as a father would a small child. Who is taller, you atop God, your Father, or Mount Everest in all its earthly magnitude?

Micah 4:1 (NASB) describes "the mountain of the house of the LORD," of which you became a member when you placed your faith in God through Jesus Christ, who "will be established as the chief of the mountains." Therefore, the house where you reside spiritually is taller than even the world's highest mountain peak.

The One in whose house you live and on whose shoulders you sit has made Himself your *sure* salvation. You are an inseparable part of His family, and His house is now your house.

As you look toward eternity, do not fear, because if you have trusted in Jesus, you will be spending it with Him.

▶ **REFLECT** How can I help someone overcome the doubts they may have about the certainty of their salvation?

▶ **PRAY** Father, continuously reveal the reality of my salvation. Show me Your plan throughout Scripture of Jesus being prophesied, then being born on the earth, then demonstrating Your Father's heart of love and ultimately dying for my sins. Show me how to ground myself in this truth so that nothing and no one can ever shake my faith's foundation.

▶ **DECLARE** Jesus has given me sure salvation.

▶ **ACT** Share your testimony of faith with someone. As you proclaim His goodness, the Holy Spirit will bear witness with your human spirit, making your awareness of your salvation even more tangible.

48 When Your Heart Is Anxious

> Say to those who have an anxious heart, "Be strong; fear not! Behold, your God will come with vengeance, with the recompense of God. He will come and save you."
>
> Isaiah 35:4 ESV

Have you recently experienced an anxious heart—one that is worried, uneasy or nervous about situations you cannot control? If you are struggling with anxiety, know that God offers you a way out of fear and into peace.

As humans, we all experience anxiety at different times in our lives. The people of Israel were no exception. They were facing a moment of weakened hands and knees because of their present adversity. Their anxiety was overtaking their prayer and worship, and they were running low on hope for a better future. Seeing their despair, God sent the prophet Isaiah to give them the great news of hope for a brighter future. God encouraged them by reminding them that He was their Vindicator, Rewarder and Savior.

In the midst of your adversity or lack of clarity, you might feel that it is the end of your future, but the truth is, your future is brighter than ever! Do not allow your heart to be troubled. Be strong and know that God is on your side. He will vindicate and reward you with His salvation.

Overcome anxiety by focusing on God and trusting in His power to rescue you. Your future is in His hands!

▶ **REFLECT** What triggers anxiety in my heart that I need God's help to overcome?

▶ **PRAY** Father God, thank You for coming into my situation with me today. Lord, I know You are my Vindicator, my Rewarder and my Savior. Please help me trust You no matter what happens. Empower me to be strong and not fear my adversity. Give me a strong mind to overcome anxiety. Help me put my focus only on You always.

▶ **DECLARE** My future is bright, and my best days are ahead!

▶ **ACT** Raise your hands and celebrate with joyful praise the victory that God is winning for you, focusing your mind and energy on His glorious power and strength.

49 The One Who Chose You

> So do not fear, for I am with you; do not be dismayed, for
> I am your God. I will strengthen you and help you; I will
> uphold you with my righteous right hand.
>
> Isaiah 41:10 NIV

God tells you to take courage, not because there are no threats against you, but because He is infinitely greater than any threat. You do not need to fear anyone or anything because *He* is your God.

Before God tells us not to fear, He shows us we can trust Him. The "so" in "so do not fear" points us back to the awe-inspiring evidence of God's power and character in Isaiah 40 and 41. His Word stands forever, while man's glory is like quickly withering grass. He "carries [us] close to his heart" as a gentle shepherd (Isaiah 40:11 NIV) and gives us strength when we are weary. He subdues earthly kingdoms, turning them to dust. He makes man-made idols look like a pathetic joke—while men nail down wobbly idols so they don't topple, He holds the universe in His steady hands, calling out each star by name.

When you compare the God who is with you to the threats against you, there is no comparison. The God who chose you is infinitely more powerful than anyone and anything, and with Him by your side, you do not need to fear.

▶ **REFLECT** In what circumstance will meditating on God's greatness help me to overcome fear?

▶ **PRAY** Father God, how awesome it is that I worship the One who created the stars and calls them each by name! Thank You for adopting me into Your family and for promising to help and uphold me when I am afraid. Help me to trust You more as I consider Your great power against evil forces and Your great love for me.

▶ **DECLARE** The One who created the stars is with me.

▶ **ACT** Take five minutes in nature gazing at or pondering the intricacies of God's creation. Consider that the Creator of all you see has promised to be with you.

50

He Holds Your Hand

> For I, the LORD your God, hold your right hand; it is I who
> say to you, "Fear not, I am the one who helps you."
>
> Isaiah 41:13 ESV

Holding another person's hand is a powerful gesture. When you experience it, you instantly understand what it represents—that you are not alone.

When a small child feels unsure or afraid, the first thing she will do is reach for her parent's hand. Once their hands are clasped together, she feels safe and secure. The danger may still be present. But she knows now that she is not alone and that there is someone stronger than herself who can protect and help her.

When the people of Israel were taken into Babylonian captivity, God sent the prophet Isaiah to assure them that, despite their dire situation, they were not alone. Even though they had rebelled against Him and made mistakes, He told them not to be afraid. He was still with them. In fact, He was so close to them, He was holding their right hand.

This promise is also for you today. You may be afraid that Jesus will not help you because of mistakes you have made, but God does not change. He still holds your hand,

and with all the powers of the universe at His command, He says, "Fear not, I am the one who helps you."

▶ **REFLECT** In what past situations have I felt the Lord holding my hand?

▶ **PRAY** Faithful God, sometimes my circumstances make me feel helpless and afraid, especially if I think I have caused the trouble myself. Thank You for holding my hand and promising to help me no matter what I have or have not done. I am so grateful that Your love is unconditional and that You always see me as Your chosen child.

▶ **DECLARE** God is holding my hand.

▶ **ACT** Find a picture of two people holding hands. Keep it where it will remind you that God is with you, giving help and comfort as He holds your right hand.

51

Your Creator Will Help You

> This is what Yahweh who made you, and formed you from the womb, who will help you says: "Don't be afraid, Jacob my servant; and you, Jeshurun, whom I have chosen."
>
> Isaiah 44:2 WEB

Have you ever feared that you lacked true worth and purpose? In His Word, God reveals this fear as a lie. If the Creator of everything made you, how can you be anything less than unique, valuable and purposeful?

Here Isaiah uses God's most holy name, Yahweh, to illustrate that God Himself created Israel by His own hand. As believers, our reverence for the gestation process from conception to birth is due largely to the idea that God Himself is intimately involved in the creation and development of every human being.

As amazing as this is, God went even further than creation, committing to help the people of Jacob and now those of us who are "in Christ," or followers of Jesus. God is One who never changes; He is the same yesterday, today and forever. Just as He formed and helped His people millennia ago, so will He help you, His precious, unique daughter or son.

God created you, knows you intimately and wants to be your Source of help in a world where fears abound; all you have to do is let Him lead as He makes the impossible possible.

▶ **REFLECT** How has God used a unique talent, interest or characteristic of mine for His glory?

▶ **PRAY** Father God, help me see myself from Your perspective, not the perspective of the world around me. Let my sense of personal worth and value be derived from what Jesus did for me on the cross, not the opinions of others. Reveal to me the magnitude of Your love for me today.

▶ **DECLARE** God Himself formed me in the womb.

▶ **ACT** Ask a friend or family member to tell you how they have seen God use your uniqueness for His glory.

52

He Has Called You by Name

Now, this is what Yahweh says: "Listen, Jacob, to the One who created you, Israel, to the One who shaped who you are. Do not fear, for I, your Kinsman-Redeemer, will rescue you. I have called you by name, and you are mine."

Isaiah 43:1 TPT

It is easy to feel fearful and alone if you believe God saved you at one point in time only to leave you on your own. The truth, though, is that God has never stopped working in your life!

You may be able to pinpoint the time and place you became a Christian, but God did not finish all His work then and there. God's work in your life is not only a historical event, but an ongoing process.

Two verbs in this verse contain the sense of something that was cut out of unshaped material but is still being worked on. The word *created*, or *bara*, is often used of wood that is cut, then shaped and polished. The word *shaped*, or *yasar*, is used when a lump of clay is formed into a vessel or a child is formed in the womb.

God's call on your life is not random. He placed you in this time and place for a reason, and He is using your surroundings, your circumstances and the people in your life to make you more like Jesus.

Like that clay on the wheel, surrender to the Master's hands, taking courage because He knows you, loves you and is not finished with you yet.

▶ **REFLECT** How have I seen the *process* of God's call on my life?

▶ **PRAY** Father, thank You for saving me and joining me to Your church. I praise You that You are not finished with me yet, but You will carry on working in my life until the very day when all Your work is finished and You lift me to a higher place. I surrender to Your shaping and refining process.

▶ **DECLARE** I am God's wonderful work in progress!

▶ **ACT** Take a few minutes and picture yourself as a lump of clay that is being shaped on the Potter's wheel. Share with someone what you see being formed.

53 God Is Pursuing You

Don't be afraid, for I am with you. I will bring your offspring from the east, and gather you from the west.

Isaiah 43:5 WEB

A man who pursues the woman he *knows* he wants to marry is a great example of God's love for you. God pursues you with the same sureness, and you never need to fear that His feelings will change.

In Isaiah 43:5, God was pursuing the love of His people, reassuring them of how precious they were to Him in spite of their shortcomings. They had had some failures because of their stubbornness and disobedience, but God was still pursuing them with His unconditional love. They were feeling displaced and perhaps insignificant, but God was after their love and lavishing His loving mercy on them. The image of God gathering His people from all corners of the earth shows us how determined God is to actively and intentionally pursue our love as a man pursues his future wife.

If God is after you, it means He really is with you and for you. He wants you to know you are precious, loved and sought after by *Him* in spite of any weaknesses or ugliness you might see in yourself.

Consider how a relationship with God is like a romantic courtship. He is intentionally pursuing you with His steadfast love and will keep you secure in that love forever.

▶ **REFLECT** How have I experienced God pursuing me?

▶ **PRAY** Father, thank You for Your unconditional love. Lord, I need to feel Your love today. Help me understand that Your love is more stubborn than my shortcomings. Teach me how to embrace Your love when I feel I don't deserve it. Open my eyes to understand Your eternal love toward me.

▶ **DECLARE** God is pursuing me with His unconditional love!

▶ **ACT** Write down the ways God has pursued you this week and share them with a friend.

The Only Rock

> "Do not tremble; do not be afraid. Did I not proclaim my
> purposes for you long ago? You are my witnesses—is there
> any other God? No! There is no other Rock—not one!"
>
> Isaiah 44:8 NLT

Some fears are so intense they make you feel as though the ground beneath you is crumbling. At times like these, remember that the Lord is your Rock, the only steady, unshakable place to stand.

Many of us respond to fear with instant action, scrambling in our own strength to build the solid rock for which we long. We toil and strive and strategize to secure a "constant" in the form of financial security, accomplishments or a relationship, only to find that the ground continues to crumble.

The idol makers described in Isaiah 44 are a prime example of how toiling to create a rock other than God is futile. The blacksmith carefully forged his idols in the fire, and the carpenter carved intricate figures from the cedar he planted and chopped himself, yet their gods had no power to save.

How much time and energy do you expend striving to create solid ground when you already have the only Rock you need—the eternal God who "does not change like shifting shadows" (James 1:17 NIV)? The next time fear strikes, instead of running to a job, achievement or person for your security, stand still and feel the firm Rock who is already beneath your feet.

▶ **REFLECT** In what area do I need to stand upon God as my Rock?

▶ **PRAY** Father God, in a world that is constantly shifting, thank You for being the unchangeable Rock beneath my feet. When I'm tempted to find security in anything other than You, remind me that no earthly wealth, accomplishment or relationship compares to what You offer. Please keep my mind, heart and body secure in You as I face today's fears, responsibilities and decisions.

▶ **DECLARE** God is my Rock.

▶ **ACT** Stand to your feet and focus on the firmness of the ground beneath you. Reflect on how God gives you the same firm place to stand in times of trouble.

55 Only God's Opinion Matters

> "Listen to me, you who know right from wrong, you who cherish my law in your hearts. Do not be afraid of people's scorn, nor fear their insults."
>
> Isaiah 51:7 NLT

From now until eternity, people will have an opinion of you, but there is only one opinion that matters.

We live in a world where people are consumed by others' lives and approval. This insatiable desire to see, know and be accepted causes people to live in a constant state of discontent, dissatisfaction and depression. There are times when we allow what other people think to carry eternal weight, but we shouldn't. The Bible explicitly commands us not to fear what others think of us.

We have been trained by society, and even the Church, to care about others' opinions, but none of those opinions matter more than God's. The prophet Isaiah reminds us to posture our heart toward God's opinions, not the opinions of others. When others' opinions are of the utmost importance, we live in fear, but when God's opinion is the most important, we experience great freedom.

Ask God to deliver you from the fear of what people think of you. God orders and orchestrates your life, and sometimes what He does will make no sense to those around you. This is when trusting God's opinion is the most vital.

Regardless of what others think, walk forward in courage, confident that God knows better than anyone what is best for your life.

▶ **REFLECT** When has knowing God's opinion of me given me courage to do something that others might not approve of?

▶ **PRAY** Father, help me to refocus my attention on the words that come from Your mouth and Your Word. Deliver me from the opinions of men. Help me only perform for an audience of one, that is You. May I be satisfied with what You say about me. God, help me not to be moved by the persecution or praise of others.

▶ **DECLARE** God's opinion of me is the most important.

▶ **ACT** Do one important thing today that you have been avoiding out of the fear of others' opinions.

56

Freedom from Shame

> "Do not be afraid; you will not be put to shame. Do not fear disgrace; you will not be humiliated. You will forget the shame of your youth and remember no more the reproach of your widowhood."
>
> Isaiah 54:4 NIV

If you had a "past" before you knew Jesus, the devil might whisper that you're not really forgiven. When the enemy taunts, declare the truth: Because of Jesus' great love, you do not need to fear God's judgment.

Isaiah 54 compares God's people to a woman who would have felt ashamed and unworthy of love because of the cultural standards of her time. In the same way, you may feel that the shame of your past defines who you are, that it is an unerasable stain that will mar your relationship with God forever.

Nothing could be further from the truth! Before God tells us we will forget our shame, He tells us *why*. Isaiah 53 prophesies of the One who removed our shame by being shamed Himself. Jesus was rejected by His people, condemned to a disgraceful death and "assigned a grave with the wicked" (Isaiah 53:9 NIV), all for us!

You do not need to live under the weight of shame, because Jesus willingly, joyfully took the burden on Himself. Because of His great love, you can walk forward in freedom with your head held high, confident and unashamed.

▶ **REFLECT** In what area does God want to set me free from shame?

▶ **PRAY** Jesus, thank You for a love so deep that You bore my shame to set me free. May I not believe the lie that You did this out of obligation, but may I understand the joy that filled Your actions. And may I live before Your face with that same joy, free from shame and confident in Your love.

▶ **DECLARE** God has freed me from shame.

▶ **ACT** Write down something you feel ashamed about, then destroy the piece of paper you wrote on as a reminder that Jesus has destroyed your shame.

57

Deliverance from Oppression and Fear

> "In righteousness you shall be established; you shall be far from oppression, for you shall not fear; and from terror, for it shall not come near you."
>
> Isaiah 54:14 ESV

This prophetic statement offers a spiritual reality available to every believer since the resurrection of Jesus.

Oppression, fear and terror still threaten the lives of many, yet God's delivering power is available through the ever-abiding presence of His Holy Spirit. His power can so permeate our physical surroundings that the present dangers, which still include oppression, fear and terror, are made impotent.

Despite being exposed to life-threatening risk, countless individuals have held fast to their active faith in God, which gave them feelings of overwhelming peace, supernatural deliverance from harm and escape from being taken hostage by fear.

Our righteousness in Christ is so all-encompassing that, at the mention of His name, situations that should produce fear, result in oppression or trigger terror are often eliminated simply because He is with us and in us. Even for those who continuously wrestle with the power of fear, the effects of oppression and the impacts of terror, the chastisement Jesus received at Calvary makes supernatural peace available to all who seek it from Him.

If oppression has put fear or terror in your heart, look to your Savior with a spirit of hope, knowing that He will deliver you in His way and in His time.

▶ **REFLECT** When I am confronted by fear, oppression and terror, what should I do?

▶ **PRAY** Father, reveal to me the reality of Your presence with me and within me. I know You will never leave or forsake me, but You will help me to bring that reality to bear on situations I face daily. As in 2 Kings 6:16, let me see with spiritual eyes that there are more with me than there are against me.

▶ **DECLARE** God will deliver me from oppression, fear and terror.

▶ **ACT** Find a ministry whose goal it is to free people from oppression (slavery, human trafficking, addiction), and contribute to that ministry through giving, praying or volunteering your time.

58 When You Feel Unqualified

"Do not say, 'I am only a youth'; for to all to whom I send you, you shall go, and whatever I command you, you shall speak. Do not be afraid of them, for I am with you to deliver you, declares the LORD."

Jeremiah 1:7–8 ESV

Feeling unqualified or intimidated before a challenge is a normal human experience, especially if others seem better qualified. The good news is that God often chooses those who are less qualified because they will need to foster a greater dependency on *Him*.

Jeremiah felt he was too young and inexperienced to fulfill God's calling on his life, but it ultimately wasn't about Jeremiah's ability, but God's empowerment. God told him not to focus on his inadequacy or be afraid of people, but instead to trust and do what *He* commanded him to do, for *He* would be with him to protect him. Although Jeremiah faced intense challenges, God was with him every step of the way, and He used him mightily as His mouthpiece to the nation of Israel.

When God calls you, it is because He has already chosen you. If He called you, He also gives you the ability to perform the task.

No matter what age you are when God calls you to do something out of your comfort zone, fear not; you can trust that *He* will empower you to do it. Know that *He* will carry out all His plans through your life as you trust and depend on *Him*.

▶ **REFLECT** The next time I feel intimidated or unqualified before a challenge, what is one way to respond that shows confidence that God will empower me?

▶ **PRAY** Father God, thank You for choosing me for Your plans. I know You love to choose the unlikely. Lord, teach me to trust You before the challenging times of my life when I might feel unqualified. Please help me depend on Your empowerment rather than focusing on my lack.

▶ **DECLARE** God uses the unlikely.

▶ **ACT** Today, be intentional by taking action on a challenging endeavor with total dependence on God. Do what God is asking you to do.

Scarecrows in a Cucumber Field

> "Their idols are like scarecrows in a cucumber field, and they cannot speak; they have to be carried, for they cannot walk. Do not be afraid of them, for they cannot do evil, neither is it in them to do good."
>
> Jeremiah 10:5 ESV

Did you ever see a scarecrow as a child and feel frightened? Today, scarecrows probably no longer frighten you. Although they may still look scary, you now know they cannot harm you.

Can you imagine how upsetting it was for the Lord to have to teach kindergarten-level spiritual principles to the nation of Israel? After all, this was a nation that had seen all the gods of Egypt humiliated—the river god, the water god, the god who was Pharaoh himself—all of these and more were brought to nothing by the true God of heaven.

Although we might not worship idols of wood or stone, an idol can also be anything or anyone that we place ahead of the true and living God: a child, a spouse or potential partner, a job or a business venture. When we believe that obtaining these things will bring us true satisfaction or that losing them will ruin our life, we have fallen for powerless, lifeless scarecrows in a cucumber field.

Do not fear any such idols, but rather worship only the living God who is worthy of awe and reverence. Only He can fill your life with the meaning, love and power for which you long.

▶ **REFLECT** What "scarecrow in a cucumber field" am I fearing today, rather than trusting in the true and living God?

▶ **PRAY** Father, educate me spiritually so that I never give anything in my life a higher value or priority than You. Show me if there are any idols in my life that I need to remove, and if there are, help me to tear them down. May You be the only One I worship.

▶ **DECLARE** Only God is worthy of my worship and awe.

▶ **ACT** Share one of your "scarecrows" with a friend or family member and brainstorm one or two practical actions you can take to remove it from its godlike status in your life.

60 A Flourishing Tree

> "They will be like a tree planted by the water that sends out its roots by the stream. It does not fear when heat comes; its leaves are always green. It has no worries in a year of drought and never fails to bear fruit."
>
> Jeremiah 17:8 NIV

When fear strikes, to whom do you run first? People can only provide momentary relief from your fears, but when you rely on God, He unleashes a steady, supernatural courage in your life.

Jeremiah contrasts two people—one who trusts in others and one who trusts in the Lord (see Jeremiah 17:5–8). The one who trusts in people shrivels like a "bush in the wastelands," and in seeking strength from others, ultimately ends up alone (verse 6 NIV). The one who trusts in the Lord, though, is like a flourishing tree that continues to blossom and bear fruit in the harshest of elements.

We can actively put our confidence in the Lord through meditating on Scriptures that speak to His character, by choosing to worship when we feel weak and by resting from our work as a symbol of our reliance on Him. As we put our confidence into practice, we will see that through our ups and downs, He is the constant Source of life, who nourishes and steadies us, whatever comes.

Put your confidence in the Lord; you can trust Him! He will give you what you need, not only to survive, but to bear fruit in your wilderness.

▶ **REFLECT** In what "wasteland" in my life do I see God producing fruit?

▶ **PRAY** Father, I confess that when things get difficult, I often seek nourishment in things that cannot give me strength. You are my only true Provider and Sustainer, the only One who can make me like a well-watered tree in the middle of a desert. As I put my confidence in You, may I bear fruit where You have planted me.

▶ **DECLARE** God makes me flourish in the wasteland.

▶ **ACT** Listen to and/or sing a song that reminds you of God's provision and faithfulness.

God Is the Ruling Authority

> "Do not fear the king of Babylon, of whom you are afraid. Do not fear him, declares the Lord, for I am with you, to save you and to deliver you from his hand."
>
> Jeremiah 42:11 ESV

Have you ever been fearful of someone in authority?

Many of us don't think we are afraid of those in leadership. We may chalk our stress and anxiety up to having a strong work ethic or serving a tough leader. But if we are honest with ourselves, we are often motivated to work hard primarily because we are afraid of what our authorities may think of us or do to us.

But fear is the antithesis of faith. We must be so committed to God in work and service that we reject the fear of our authorities when it surfaces. If fear of how we may be treated makes us apprehensive of work and service environments, something is wrong.

If we need to leave a toxic, unhealthy environment, we can fully trust in God's provision. But if we carry fear of authority with us regardless of our working environment, we need to evaluate whether we are fully trusting God with our self-worth and livelihood.

You never need to fear those in leadership because God is the ultimate ruling authority. As you submit this fear to Him, you will begin to experience the joy that comes from working for the Lord and not for people.

▶ **REFLECT** How can I respond the next time I experience fear of someone in a leadership role over me?

▶ **PRAY** Father, thank You for having charge of the universe and for delivering me from fear. Your Word declares that I don't have to fear man, and Your Word is true! You are my light and salvation. I am confident You will take care of me. Give me courage to operate in faith and not fear.

▶ **DECLARE** I work for the Lord, not for people.

▶ **ACT** Anonymously do something kind for those in leadership over you, whether they are good or bad leaders, doing it as unto the Lord.

62 God Chastises Those Whom He Cherishes

> "Do not be afraid, Jacob my servant, for I am with you," declares the LORD. "Though I completely destroy all the nations among which I scatter you, I will not completely destroy you. I will discipline you but only in due measure; I will not let you go entirely unpunished."
>
> Jeremiah 46:28 NIV

Have you ever felt like God was mad at you because of how He disciplined you?

Every child of God will experience God's discipline. Humanistic wisdom views discipline as negative, and Satan and enemies of the cross depict it as punishment, but discipline is actually God's training.

God is a good Father, not an evil taskmaster. Hebrews 12:6 declares that God chastises every son whom He loves. God loves us and wants us to be righteous and holy, so He orchestrates our lives so that we learn to obey Him. God's discipline is not punitive, but it is often protective—not allowing us to get what we desperately desire because it would be destructive to our lives.

At times, it's God's correction or allowing us to reap from our own harvest. During seasons when we reap the consequences of our actions, God still loves us, grants us mercy and keeps us from being tried beyond our capacity.

You never have to fear God's chastisement, for through it, He is demonstrating His fatherhood in your life. Parents want the best for their children and are often creative in how they achieve that. As your heavenly Father, God will continue to use creative ways to help you become more like Jesus.

▶ **REFLECT** How has God's discipline helped me to become more like Jesus?

▶ **PRAY** Father, I repent for seeing You negatively and for believing the lies of the devil. You are loving in Your correction and discipline. Thank You for desiring that I become more like You. Help me, God, to be like You. God, grant me grace and mercy when I reap the consequences of my own choices. Help me to embrace Your chastisement.

▶ **DECLARE** God disciplines those whom He loves.

▶ **ACT** Ask a fellow believer to share a time when God disciplined them for their own good.

63

Stand Up

> Then he continued, "Do not be afraid, Daniel. Since the first
> day that you set your mind to gain understanding and to
> humble yourself before your God, your words were heard,
> and I have come in response to them."
>
> Daniel 10:12 NIV

Has shame over your sinfulness ever made you hesitant to
approach God in prayer? Remember that when you stand
before God, He sees you, His beloved child, and delights in
answering you with wisdom and grace.

After Daniel received a disturbing vision, he fasted and
prayed for wisdom for three weeks. In answer to his prayer,
a luminous man in bright clothes came to deliver a message.
Some Bible scholars say he was an angel; some say he was
Jesus Himself. But in any case, his glory terrified Daniel, who
felt unworthy to stand before him.

The man's words to Daniel are key for our prayer lives:
"Daniel, you who are highly esteemed, consider carefully
the words I am about to speak to you, and *stand up*, for
I have now been sent to you" (Daniel 10:11 NIV, emphasis
added). God is pleased by our humble pursuit of wisdom,
and He invites us to stand up, confident in His eternal love

and His promise to give us the wisdom we have asked for (see James 1:5).

Do not fear approaching God in prayer. Like Daniel, stand up and receive the wisdom that God delights in giving you.

▶ **REFLECT** In what situation do I need to boldly ask God for wisdom?

▶ **PRAY** Father, sometimes the awareness of all the ways I fall short of Your glory makes me afraid to approach You. Holy Spirit, extinguish this fear and replace it with the confidence that I am pleasing to God because of what Jesus has done, so that I may boldly approach the throne of grace as a child runs to her father.

▶ **DECLARE** God loves to give me wisdom.

▶ **ACT** The next time you pray, stand up just as the glorious man told Daniel to do as a sign of confidence in God's love and desire to give you the wisdom you seek.

64

Precious to God

> "Don't be afraid," he said, "for you are very precious to God. Peace! Be encouraged! Be strong!" As he spoke these words to me, I suddenly felt stronger and said to him, "Please speak to me, my lord, for you have strengthened me."
>
> Daniel 10:19 NLT

Take a moment and marvel at the truth that the God who spoke the universe into being speaks to you. Meditating on how precious you are to God will strengthen you and break fear and discouragement.

Stunned by the glory of the angelic messenger, Daniel felt so faint he could barely speak. But suddenly, Daniel felt stronger and was ready to listen. What sparked this sudden strength? Daniel's fears fled when the messenger told him he was "very precious to God." The knowledge of God's love grounded Daniel, putting him in the right mindset to listen and fulfill the task God had called him to do.

Daniel's response is a beautiful illustration of the apostle John's declaration that "there is no fear in love. But perfect love drives out fear, because fear has to do with punishment" (1 John 4:18 NIV). Knowing that he was loved banished any fear Daniel had of punishment and replaced it with holy strength.

The more you reflect on the truth that God cherishes you, the clearer you will see things, the stronger you will feel and the more courage you will have to do what He has called you to do.

▶ **REFLECT** In what area do I need God's perfect love to drive out my fear?

▶ **PRAY** Jesus, I stand in awe of Your great love, a love so deep and unyielding that You went to the cross for me. When I fall prey to deceit and doubt Your love, banish the lies and replace them with the truth. Strengthen me with a deep understanding of Your love, and may that strength be used to Your glory.

▶ **DECLARE** God's perfect love strengthens me.

▶ **ACT** Start a list of all the evidence in your life that you are precious to God.

65 Rejoice in the Lord

> Don't be afraid, O land. Be glad now and rejoice, for the
> LORD has done great things.
>
> Joel 2:21 NLT

Have you or someone you know ever needed urgent medical help? Sometimes fear strikes with the same sense of urgency. Throughout His Word, God says that rejoicing is the perfect emergency antidote whenever you feel overcome by fear.

Fear is a rational response when we are facing life-threatening danger or pain. Fear becomes debilitating, however, when it paralyzes our hope and we no longer experience the peace and joy of the Lord. We can feel helpless under its suffocating power.

In Joel 2:21, we are given an effective antidote for every form of fear. We are told to rejoice because "the LORD has done great things." The word *great* means "unlimited, boundless, vast, immense." God does great things because He Himself is great, and He loves doing miraculous works—big and small—to show mercy to His people and make our hearts glad.

Rejoicing in the great things God has done for you will free you from fear's paralyzing grip. Genuine gladness and anxiety cannot coexist. When you celebrate God's many kindnesses to you, even when life feels hard, fear gives way to peace and hope—like darkness gives way to light or silence to a beautiful song.

▶ **REFLECT** What great things has God done in my life that give me reason to rejoice?

▶ **PRAY** Holy Spirit, please help me to see the greatness of God so that I can be glad today. I admit that my troubles can often consume me and make it difficult to rejoice. Knowing You are with me and always doing great things gives me new joy. Give me Your grace to walk in this gladness every day.

▶ **DECLARE** Rejoicing in God's great works frees me from fear.

▶ **ACT** Creatively celebrate in some way something God has done in your life lately.

God Will Restore

> Don't be afraid, you animals of the field, for the wilderness
> pastures will soon be green. The trees will again be filled
> with fruit; fig trees and grapevines will be loaded down
> once more.
>
> Joel 2:22 NLT

Have you ever returned to a place you enjoyed in your past
only to discover it is now run-down and of little use? Or
possibly you know what it feels like to live with depleted
assets or reaping the consequences of bad past choices?

We all have been in dry, dark seasons of our lives when
we think there is no hope. This lack of hope often leads to
fear—fear that God has forgotten us and that things will
always be this way. The people of God were experiencing
such a time of desolation as their crops were eaten up by
locusts. He had not forgotten His people, though. God, who
is rich in mercy, gracious and slow to anger, was waiting for
the hearts of His people to turn to Him. As they turned to
Him, the trees again would be filled with fruit.

God desires to restore us to Himself before restoring our
material blessings. When God allows times of hardship, He
is calling us to go deeper with *Him*.

Fear wants to cripple you during those hard times, but God's gracious and merciful love is what turns your hardships into unexplainable joy and an abundance of blessings. And the first blessing He wants to give you is a deeper relationship with *Him*.

▶ **REFLECT** Have I ever experienced a dry season in my life? What did I learn about God during that season?

▶ **PRAY** Father, thank You for Your grace. Lord, please help me discern what You would have me learn in this season. I know You are calling me to go deeper and that You will turn my hardship into a time of restoration and abundance. Show me Your will for my life. Restore my blessings.

▶ **DECLARE** God will restore every blessing.

▶ **ACT** Plant a seed or buy a small plant or flower; each time you water it, reflect on the growth God is producing in your life.

67 No Retreat, No Surrender

> On that day they will say to Jerusalem, "Do not fear, Zion; do not let your hands hang limp. The Lord your God is with you, the Mighty Warrior who saves. He will take great delight in you; in his love he will no longer rebuke you, but will rejoice over you with singing."
>
> Zephaniah 3:16–17 NIV

Satan is a masterful deceiver, and he wants to fill your mind with lies so you will retreat from God's love and surrender your faith. But you don't need to fear Satan's power, for he is subject to God.

God fights with us and for us. Psalm 24:8 declares our God to be mighty in battle. Our God is a mighty warrior; with Him we win all fights. The strategy of the enemy is to convince us that fear is real so we will surrender to his antics. He wants us to believe we are helpless. He wants our hands to be limp and not ready for battle.

Satan wants us to retreat from our position of power and love and surrender to fear. Remember that the devil is the father of lies. When Satan lies to you about being weak, boldly declare your strength and fight the fight of faith.

The next time the devil attacks you with fear in the midst of your faith-fight, declare, "I will not retreat, nor will I surrender." God is your mighty warrior; He loves you and takes great delight in you. You don't have to retreat or surrender anything to the evil one.

▶ **REFLECT** How have I seen God act as a mighty warrior on my behalf?

▶ **PRAY** Heavenly Father, thank You for being my fortress and shield. Thank You for being my battle-axe. Remind me that You will always cause me to triumph. Help me to walk victoriously in every battle. Teach my hands to war and not to hang limp. Teach me how to effectively use the whole armor of God.

▶ **DECLARE** God is a mighty warrior against every lie.

▶ **ACT** Consider whether you've given up in any area of your life. Then, with a trusted friend, discuss how to reengage in that area.

The Holy Spirit Is in You

> "Be strong, all you people of the land," declares the LORD,
> "and work. For I am with you," declares the LORD Almighty.
> "This is what I covenanted with you when you came out
> of Egypt. And my Spirit remains among you. Do not fear."
>
> Haggai 2:4–5 NIV

Is God calling you to something beyond your ability? Fear of failure may tempt you to abandon your calling, but with God, your insufficiencies are irrelevant—the Holy Spirit dwells *in* you and will empower you.

The book of Haggai opens with a discouraged, passive remnant—although God had brought His people out of exile, they had postponed the completion of the temple out of fear and self-preservation. The prophet Haggai rouses them to action with a command filled with encouragement—they must continue the work God has called them to do, and His Spirit will remain among them. Freed from fear, the people joyfully obey and resume their work.

God's steady presence *among* the people of Israel as they rebuilt the temple was glorious. Even more glorious, though, is that today, all believers are *indwelt* by the Holy

Spirit. God's people are no longer building the temple with the Spirit among them, but they are *themselves* the temple of the Holy Spirit.

As you bravely obey God's call on your life, know you are never alone. Not only is God with you, but the Holy Spirit lives in you, empowering you to do impossible things.

▶ **REFLECT** How have I recently experienced the Holy Spirit working in my life?

▶ **PRAY** Holy Spirit, much of my fear stems from forgetting that You indwell and empower me to complete the work I am called to do. Where I am weak, show Your strength, and where I am afraid, inspire me to boldness so that Your power and glory will shine through me to this dark world.

▶ **DECLARE** The Holy Spirit indwells and empowers me.

▶ **ACT** Notice and document when the Holy Spirit within you nudges you and influences your thoughts and actions so that you can cultivate a greater awareness of Him in and around you.

69 Be a Blessing

> "Among the other nations, Judah and Israel became symbols of a cursed nation. But no longer! Now I will rescue you and make you both a symbol and a source of blessing. So don't be afraid. Be strong, and get on with rebuilding the Temple!"
>
> Zechariah 8:13 NLT

If you have ever received a special favor, mercy or benefit from someone, then you know what a blessing is. God desires to bless others through you. This wonderful truth helps fear of the tasks before you to fade.

The people of God had become a cursed nation due to their sin, but God is merciful and wanted to give the remnant of Israel and Judah another chance because of His goodness and faithful promises. "You were a cursed nation, but no longer!" the Lord told them. All they needed now was not to fear, but rather to be strong and get on with the task of rebuilding the temple. They were now to become a symbol and a source of blessing to all the nations.

God is the only One who can make you both a symbol and a source of blessings. God wants to bless you and make you a channel of His blessing to others. Sometimes fear of the task, fear of people or fear of failure can get in the way of this. When fear comes, remember that God eagerly desires for you to be a blessing, and He will certainly work through you to bless others with His love, kindness and hope.

▶ **REFLECT** When did I last take time to bless someone who did not deserve it?

▶ **PRAY** Lord, thank You for making me a symbol and a source of blessing to others. Take away my fear of people, of failure or of the task before me. By Your mercy, empower me not just to receive Your blessing, but also to be a blessing to many. Show me how I can bless others.

▶ **DECLARE** The Lord has made me a symbol and a source of blessing!

▶ **ACT** Bless someone by doing a special favor for them or showing them mercy.

70

A Courageous Trust

> But as he considered these things, behold, an angel of the
> Lord appeared to him in a dream, saying, "Joseph, son of
> David, do not fear to take Mary as your wife, for that which
> is conceived in her is from the Holy Spirit."
>
> Matthew 1:20 ESV

How do you approach a difficult decision? Do you analyze
costs and benefits, seek the counsel of others or just go
with your gut? Whatever the process, your perspective
impacts everything.

Perspective certainly mattered when it came to the circumstances of Jesus' conception, recounted in Matthew 1.
From an earthly point of view, Joseph's decision to divorce
Mary helps him avoid a damaged reputation, an unfaithful
spouse and Mary's public execution (adultery was punish-
able by stoning). Like any of us would, Joseph pursues the
course of action most likely to yield a favorable outcome.

What is humanly possible or beneficial are not the criteria
for God's plans, however. An angel draws Joseph from the
natural into the supernatural, recalibrating his version of
reality: Mary's "illegitimate" pregnancy is actually evidence
of the purest love. Trusting God's perspective over his own

enabled Joseph to set aside real probabilities and fears and play a key role in the Savior's birth.

If you are struggling to see past your circumstances or make a difficult decision, be encouraged to seek God's perspective. The Holy Spirit may not reveal all the details, but His plans can be trusted. Fears and impossibilities will fade as you invite heaven to come to earth.

▶ **REFLECT** In what area do I need to let the Holy Spirit influence my perspective on life?

▶ **PRAY** Holy Spirit, I am amazed at Your willingness to share Your perspective and include me in Your plans. Thank You for helping Joseph overcome his fears and make room for Jesus. Help me do the same. When facing difficult decisions and situations, I want to value Your heart and Your revelation above everything else.

▶ **DECLARE** I can trust God's perspective and plans.

▶ **ACT** Encourage someone who is facing a dilemma or difficult decision with perspective and hope from God's Word.

71

A New Perspective

> Then the angel spoke to the women. "Don't be afraid!" he
> said. "I know you are looking for Jesus, who was crucified.
> He isn't here! He is risen from the dead, just as he said
> would happen. Come, see where his body was lying."
>
> Matthew 28:5–6 NLT

Imagine going into a funeral home to pay your respects, only to find that your loved one is no longer there. Through His empty tomb, Jesus proves His power to accomplish His promises, offering you a new perspective on your fears.

Two women approached Jesus' grave early that morning, expecting to see a large stone blocking their entry. They had witnessed their Lord's gruesome death and wept as His lifeless body was laid on the tomb's cold stone slab. From their perspective, Jesus' enemies had won. Now all they could do was anoint His body with spices, one last tender act of devotion and love.

But suddenly, everything changed. The earth shook beneath their feet. They heard the angel's strange and wonderful words, "Don't be afraid! He isn't here! He is risen!" As they marveled at the empty tomb, their grief transformed into incredible joy. It was just as He had said: "But after I am raised up, I will go before you to Galilee" (Mark 14:28 ESV).

When your fears are confronted by God's life-giving power, His joy will fill your heart, and your perspective will instantly change. You will no longer be afraid, for this God who raised Himself from the dead is with you today!

▶ **REFLECT** How does the resurrection of Jesus give me new perspective today?

▶ **PRAY** Risen Lord, knowing that You overcame the grave changes my perspective and fills me with new hope for my future. It may look like the enemy has won, but You have resurrection power, and You do all that You say You will do. When I am afraid, please give me a new perspective that transforms my anxiety into abundant and abiding joy.

▶ **DECLARE** Jesus' resurrection fills me with hope.

▶ **ACT** Encourage someone who is struggling with grief with the hope Jesus offers through His resurrection.

72

We Have Seen Jesus

> Suddenly Jesus met them. "Greetings," he said. They came to him, clasped his feet and worshiped him. Then Jesus said to them, "Do not be afraid. Go and tell my brothers to go to Galilee; there they will see me."
>
> Matthew 28:9–10 NIV

Do you fear sharing your faith when you are unsure of someone's response? Jesus asks you to courageously share with others so they can see and worship Him, too.

How wonderful it must have been for Mary Magdalene and Mary the mother of James to hear Jesus' familiar voice again! Only days before, they had seen His body broken and scourged, pierced with nails, spear and thorns. His closest disciples had scattered and were in hiding. But these two women had just come from the empty tomb, filled with joyful hope that their Savior was alive.

And now here He was with them, greeting them in His loving way. No one knows all they said to each other. But eventually Jesus told them what He wanted them to do next—go and tell the brothers that they would see Him in Galilee.

Would the men believe them? The testimony of women in their culture bore little weight. But knowing Jesus was with them again, the two women went to the brothers, who then traveled to Galilee and worshiped their risen Lord (see Matthew 28:16–17).

So do not be afraid! Go and tell others God is with us so that they might worship Him, too.

▶ **REFLECT** Who are the people the Holy Spirit is leading me to tell about Jesus?

▶ **PRAY** Precious Lord, I confess that I am often afraid to tell people about You, fearing their rejection or disdain. Please forgive me and give me courage because You are with me to go and share what I have seen and heard. Open my eyes to see Your love and beauty, that I may bow in humble worship.

▶ **DECLARE** Jesus gives me courage to tell others He is with us.

▶ **ACT** Ask the Holy Spirit for courage to tell one person about the Lord this week. Trust God with the person's response.

73

When It Seems Too Late

> While He was still speaking, some came from the ruler of the synagogue's house who said, "Your daughter is dead. Why trouble the Teacher any further?" As soon as Jesus heard the word that was spoken, He said to the ruler of the synagogue, "Do not be afraid; only believe."
>
> Mark 5:35–36 NKJV

When you don't receive an immediate response to your prayer, do you fear that God won't answer you in time for it to matter? Although God's timing might not be the same as your timing, He hears and will answer.

Jairus, a local synagogue leader, fell at Jesus' feet and begged Him to come and heal his dying daughter. Jesus agreed, but on His way, He was intercepted by a woman who believed that if she could just touch His clothes, she would be healed. She did and she was. Just then, devastating news arrived from the home of Jairus that his daughter had died. It seemed that Jesus was too late.

But Jesus told him not to worry, but instead believe and his dead daughter would be made well! It took an amazing level of trust for Jairus to accept such a seemingly impossible statement from Jesus, but Jairus said nothing in reply and the two of them continued to his home, where Christ raised Jairus' daughter to life.

When God's Word declares a promise and you are struggling to believe it, do not fear. Simply keep walking with Jesus, and He will do all that is necessary. Jesus is *never* too late.

▶ **REFLECT** In what area where it seems as if it is too late do I need to trust God's timing?

▶ **PRAY** Father, I thank You that with You it is never too late. It seemed too late for Sarah to give birth, for Jacob ever to see Joseph again, or for the prodigal to return home. But with You it is never too late. Help me to believe Your promises and wait for Your timing.

▶ **DECLARE** Jesus is never too late.

▶ **ACT** Ask another believer to share a testimony of how God answered a prayer when it seemed like it was too late.

74

No Counterfeit Jesus

> But when they saw him walking on the water, they cried out in terror, thinking he was a ghost. They were all terrified when they saw him. But Jesus spoke to them at once. "Don't be afraid," he said. "Take courage! I am here!"
>
> Mark 6:49–50 NLT

A deep understanding of Jesus' identity is fatal to fear. The more you comprehend Jesus' infinite strength and intimate love for you, the less power fear will wield in your life.

Fear thrives off deception, and the enemy has worked for centuries to trick us with a counterfeit version of Jesus. In our most vulnerable moments, we are often assaulted with the lies that Jesus does not know us, care for us or have the power to help us. As the lies take root, so does fear.

In Mark 6, the disciples' blindness to Jesus' identity crippled them with fear. They had just seen Jesus miraculously feed five thousand people with next to no food, but their hearts were still hardened to His deity. Although they had just seen Him work a miracle, when they saw their Rabbi again working outside the confines of human physics, they didn't recognize Him.

Jesus' exhortation to take courage because He is with you only destroys fear when you understand who He is. Reject the counterfeit version of Jesus and press into the truth that in Him, there is no condemnation, and His love for you is more powerful than anything that comes against you.

▶ **REFLECT** When have I been blind to Jesus' presence in the middle of a storm?

▶ **PRAY** Jesus, I want to know You better. Give me a greater revelation of Your love so that I may be rooted in the hope that You have called me to. Help me to see You as You are and to reject all counterfeits. I love You, Jesus; open my eyes to new depths of Your love.

▶ **DECLARE** Knowing who Jesus is frees me from fear.

▶ **ACT** Encourage someone who is struggling in their faith with an account of Jesus' work in your life.

75

Your Prayer Has Been Heard

> But the angel said to him, "Do not be afraid, Zechariah, for
> your prayer has been heard, and your wife Elizabeth will
> bear you a son, and you shall name him John."
>
> Luke 1:13 NASB

Have you ever feared that God doesn't hear your prayers? One of the enemy's chief strategies is to convince you that God doesn't hear your voice. Scripture makes it clear, though, that God *has* heard your prayers.

During desperate times when we pray for God's merciful intervention, the enemy loves to plant questions in our mind about God's involvement in our lives. "Is He listening?" "Does He hear me?" "Is my request worthy of His involvement?" We may even wonder if He functions like a supreme court of law, which first decides whether they will hear a case before the petitioners can even make their case before them.

The account of Zechariah illustrates how clearly God hears us and how willingly He responds. The angel's confident proclamation left no doubt as to whether God hears the prayers of His people.

If you ever fear that God doesn't hear you, remember you have a scriptural basis for being heard: 1 John 5:14 says, "If we ask anything according to His will, He hears us" (NASB). As you present your requests to Him, submitting them to His will, trust that He has heard your voice.

▶ **REFLECT** How would my thoughts and actions change if I was fully confident that God the Father Himself hears and responds positively to my prayers?

▶ **PRAY** Father in heaven, show me the reality that as I lift my heart to pray in faith according to Your will, which is revealed in Your Word, You will hear me. Thank You in advance for teaching me how to pray according to Your plans for me and those around me.

▶ **DECLARE** God hears every prayer I pray.

▶ **ACT** Pray something extraordinarily bold—a dream you feel God has placed on your heart but you have yet to embrace by faith.

76

Favor with God

> And the angel said to her, "Do not be afraid, Mary, for you have found favor with God."
>
> Luke 1:30 NASB

If an angel appeared to you in all his heavenly glory, you would be afraid. Do you think your response would change, though, if the angel told you that you had found favor with God?

"It would depend on what *favor* actually means," you might respond, since a second virgin birth is clearly unnecessary due to the finished work of Jesus. The word *favor* means "to pursue with grace, encompass with favor or to honor with blessings." By this definition, God's favor is a great antidote to fear.

The good news is we already have access to God's favor—we are eternally connected to the One who is truly worthy of glory, honor and praise. Once we have accepted Jesus as Savior and made Him Lord of our lives, we are supernaturally placed "in Him." We can be sure that if God's favor is upon Jesus and we are "in Christ," then God's favor flows to us by the power of His Spirit within us.

With God's favor flowing through you, you do not need to fear anyone or anything. Just as God's favor empowered Mary to follow Him, let God's favor empower you to step into His calling without fear.

▶ **REFLECT** How would my daily life change if I knew, with certainty, that I was forever favored by God?

▶ **PRAY** Father, show me how much You favor Jesus and then reveal how intimately I am connected to Him. Show me how Your love and favor flows into my life, like the sap from the vine flows into the connected branches. Make me mindful of Your favor so I can light the way for others to Your redeeming love.

▶ **DECLARE** I have favor with God.

▶ **ACT** Look for one way to show someone favor today.

77

Embrace the Good News

> And the angel said to them, "Fear not, for behold, I bring you good news of great joy that will be for all the people."
>
> Luke 2:10 ESV

When the angel said, "good news of great joy to all people," *you* were one of the people he was referencing, some two thousand years later.

Jesus' entrance into the earth as an infant was so momentous that all of heaven seemed to break through into this physical realm to proclaim the goodness and mercy of God the Father and the Holy Spirit.

Why were they so excited? The heart of the Father had long desired to rescue humankind from its bondage to fear and separation that came into being through the errors of Adam and Eve. In fact, the first thing God said in the Garden of Eden after the Fall was that One would be sent to restore our lost fellowship with God (see Genesis 3:14–15).

The fear-eliminating good news is that the God of the universe is wildly in love with His precious creation, so much so that even death on the cross and three days in the grave did not prevent Him from doing whatever was necessary to clear a path between Himself and you. Don't hold this good news at arm's length, but embrace it, and it will extinguish the power of fear in your life.

▶ **REFLECT** What good news would bring great joy for me at this point in my life?

▶ **PRAY** Father, reveal to me Your dreams for me in this life. You worked for generations to reach the moment when Jesus was safely born of a virgin on the earth. Reveal the great joy of this good news to me daily so I can walk with ever-increasing confidence in Your Word and Your ways.

▶ **DECLARE** God has good news of great joy for me.

▶ **ACT** Set an alarm for three times throughout your day today. When the alarm goes off, smile and rejoice in some way for the Good News of Jesus Christ.

78 Amazed but Not Afraid

For he and all his companions were astonished at the catch of fish they had taken, and so were James and John, the sons of Zebedee, Simon's partners. Then Jesus said to Simon, "Don't be afraid; from now on you will fish for people."

Luke 5:9–10 NIV

Can you recall your first real encounter with Jesus? Did you hear His voice or witness His provision or healing power? Whatever it was, how did you respond to experiencing Him personally?

In Luke 5, Simon Peter has an up-close encounter with Jesus. The chapter begins with Jesus using Simon's boat to teach a crowd from a distance, out on the lake. Afterward, He gives back to Simon far more than he gave; when He tells the fishermen to cast again, their nets are miraculously filled. Simon was amazed, but he was also afraid.

We, too, may have mixed feelings upon a fresh revelation of Jesus. His unlimited power and intimate knowledge of us inspires awe. His invitation to join our lives with His may trigger shame and unworthiness.

As these feelings arise, Jesus calms them. We see no place for fear as He draws Simon closer to Himself, into a higher purpose and partnership: fishing for souls with His continued direction and provision.

Jesus has the same impact today. He relates to you with grace and generosity. He calls and equips you for greater things. And while following Him may continue to cause strong reactions, fear is not meant to be one of them.

▶ **REFLECT** What is my response when Jesus does something new in my life?

▶ **PRAY** Lord Jesus, thank You for this story of Simon Peter's encounter with You. Help me not to be afraid or ashamed of Your powerful presence and gracious work in my life. I want to deepen my relationship with You and pursue the calling You have for me. Increase my faith and trust as Your disciple.

▶ **DECLARE** I will not be afraid of Jesus' work in my life.

▶ **ACT** Take one risk today for Jesus in the context of a calling on your life (workplace, ministry, relationship). Risks could include being unusually generous, offering prayer or asking for forgiveness.

Do Not Fear Death

"I tell you, my friends, do not fear those who kill the body,
and after that have nothing more that they can do."

Luke 12:4 ESV

What would you do if you had no fear? Books on self-development often challenge their readers to answer this question. Imagining a life of such freedom helps identify what really matters to you and what holds you back.

In Luke 12:4, Jesus engages His disciples in a similar exercise. He has them consider how the fear of death impacts the way they live. Faithfulness to Him above personal safety was a value system He taught more than once and one He modeled for us: Jesus' obedience to God resulted in the killing of His body. But ultimately, that body was resurrected and seated in heavenly places, beyond harm's reach. His destiny was ever eternal, ever in God's hands.

We have oneness with Jesus in our humanity. He has been down this same path and calls us His friends, naming our fears and reminding us of man's limited power. Even our worst enemies cannot do anything to us after a certain point. It is in death that a Christian's life really begins.

Jesus wants this truth to free you. What really matters is not what anyone or anything can do to end your life, but that while it lasts, you live for Him.

▶ **REFLECT** If God has destined me for eternity, what makes me fear losing my life?

▶ **PRAY** Jesus, my Friend, thank You that I am not just a body; I am a soul. Give me a greater awareness of eternity. Help me entrust my fragile life into Your hands. I give You my fears of being harmed and of dying. I want to live, without reservation, for You.

▶ **DECLARE** Jesus has conquered death.

▶ **ACT** Look up quotes and sayings about death and dying from other respected Christians (past or present). Be encouraged by their courage and heavenly perspective.

80 Finding Your Worth in God

> "Are not five sparrows sold for two pennies? Yet not one of them is forgotten by God. Indeed, the very hairs of your head are all numbered. Don't be afraid; you are worth more than many sparrows."
>
> Luke 12:6–7 NIV

Do you ever fear you are too small to be of much significance to God? In Luke 12, Jesus speaks to this fear by assuring you that you are of great worth to Him.

When we look for our worth in our accomplishments or others' opinions, we ride a roller coaster of insecurity and fear. Jesus gives us the only secure place to find our worth: knowing the great value God places on us. We alone of all creation are created in His likeness. Although being compared to sparrows may seem humbling, Jesus is giving a somewhat humorous example meant to magnify our great value to God. If He grants such worth to the smallest of His creatures by caring for them, how much more will He watch over and provide for us, His children?

But the greatest evidence of our worth is that Jesus came to die for us. "Greater love has no one than this: to lay down one's life for one's friends" (John 15:13 NIV). Even as He taught them this lesson, Jesus knew He was headed to the cross.

You can abandon your fears of insignificance; you will never be forgotten by a God who places such high value on you!

▶ **REFLECT** How can I find my worth from God instead of from other unreliable sources?

▶ **PRAY** Loving God, as the Author of all creation, You alone give me my true worth. You love me because You have chosen to do so, not because I could do anything to deserve it. Help me rest, knowing how valuable I am to You and that You care intimately about every detail of my life.

▶ **DECLARE** God highly values me.

▶ **ACT** When you see a sparrow, bird or other small animal today, let it remind you of your own great worth in God's eyes.

81 Words from the Holy Spirit

> "And when they bring you before the synagogues and the rulers and the authorities, do not be anxious about how you should defend yourself or what you should say, for the Holy Spirit will teach you in that very hour what you ought to say."
>
> Luke 12:11–12 ESV

When you face fearful circumstances in which you don't know what to say or do, remember the Holy Spirit's work. The Holy Spirit plays various roles in your life to make you a more courageous follower of Jesus.

Christ promised that His Father would send the Holy Spirit as our Comforter, or Helper, or Advocate. (Each of these titles equates to the Greek word *parakletos* used in John 14:16.)

A common fear is not sharing the Gospel clearly with those we love. Although we should be prepared to answer others' questions, we must also trust the Holy Spirit as our Helper to teach us what to say, for it is the Holy Spirit, not our eloquence or apologetics, who convicts and saves others.

When we are suffering, the Holy Spirit is our Comforter, and He speaks words of consolation to our hearts and minds.

When we are at a loss for words, the Holy Spirit is our Advocate, who gives us appropriate things to say.

Whatever you are facing, you do not need to fear saying or doing the wrong thing if you are relying on the Holy Spirit. Just be still and listen, and the Holy Spirit will speak and comfort and instruct you.

► **REFLECT** What words is the Holy Spirit speaking to me now?

► **PRAY** Father, thank You for sending me the Holy Spirit as my Comforter, Helper and Advocate. May I know His voice distinctly and listen to Him carefully. May He teach me what I should say and speak into my heart and mind when I need to be comforted, directed or helped.

► **DECLARE** The Holy Spirit comforts, teaches and defends me!

► **ACT** Ask the Holy Spirit to give you His words for a situation you encounter today. Remain attentive throughout your day to listen and respond to the Holy Spirit.

82

The Gift of the Kingdom

> "Fear not, little flock, for it is your Father's good pleasure to give you the kingdom."
>
> Luke 12:32 ESV

Have you ever had these thoughts? *God's love is too good to be true. God is disappointed in me; His grace and forgiveness are just part of a bargain, not who He really is or what He really wants.*

In the words of Jesus recorded in Luke 12, Jesus takes care to correct our misconceptions about the nature of God. After encouraging us not to worry about death, trials or daily needs, He cuts to our deepest fear as believers, perhaps the one underlying all the others: that God is more prone to judge us than be generous with us. Jesus defines the truth about God's heart and the relationship the Father has with His children. His revelation puts our fears to rest.

Let these words of Jesus set the record straight for you today. God is not an angry or begrudging authority figure. He is not waiting for you to slip up so He can punish you.

Even in your weakness and dependence, He desires to freely give you His Kingdom—all that He is and has.

In those moments of worrying or wondering how God relates to you, be reassured: Your Father delights in loving you and giving you His very best.

▶ **REFLECT** Where might I have misunderstood God's heart for me?

▶ **PRAY** Heavenly Father, I want to know who You really are. Thank You for how Jesus reveals Your relationship to me, Your child. Free me from fear of Your judgment. Help me receive Your love and Your kingdom in greater measure. I want to experience Your goodness and the pleasure You take in sharing it with me.

▶ **DECLARE** God loves to share His kingdom with me.

▶ **ACT** Look for signs of God's kingdom today (e.g., fruits of the Spirit manifested in you or others, healing, restoration, answered prayer and justice).

83

The Return of the King

> "Fear not, daughter of Zion; behold, your king is coming,
> sitting on a donkey's colt!"
>
> John 12:15 ESV

Do you ever feel as if the world is full of hopeless gloom and doom? As a believer, you do not need to fear as those without hope because King Jesus is soon returning with all power in His hands.

It is easy to believe the lies of the media, the enemies of the cross and the devil. We are constantly bombarded with negativity, tragedy and hopelessness. Sometimes we respond by wavering in our faith and accepting the bait of fear.

Fear is a very powerful emotion; it has been known to cause anxiety and even heart attacks. In Luke 21:26, the Bible says that men's hearts will literally fail because of fear. But we can rest in the knowledge that God holds our tomorrow, that our eternity is secure and that our King will return for us.

In the meantime, work faithfully and fearlessly in what God has assigned you to do. There will be onslaughts of battles from the enemy and the world, but these are temporary. You have the unshakable hope that God is with you, in this world and in the world to come.

Take heart, for King Jesus is coming soon!

▶ **REFLECT** What lies of the media, the world and the devil have I allowed to influence my peace?

▶ **PRAY** Father, I am grateful that You are the King of all kings. I am thankful that You are coming back for me. Thank You for being a faithful God. Thank You for showing me how to have faith in fearful times. Thank You for keeping my heart still and resting in Your Word. I look forward to Your return.

▶ **DECLARE** Jesus is my King, and He is returning soon.

▶ **ACT** Listen to or sing a song that sets your mind on Jesus' return.

84

Surrendering Control

> "Last night an angel of the God to whom I belong and whom
> I serve stood beside me and said, 'Do not be afraid, Paul.
> You must stand trial before Caesar; and God has graciously
> given you the lives of all who sail with you.'"
>
> Acts 27:23–24 NIV

In a world that fights fear with attempted control, God calls you to exchange control for His peace. Each of your days is in His hands, and He will fulfill His will for you.

In Acts 27, certain death appears to await Paul and his shipmates—after being battered by a violent storm, they "finally gave up all hope of being saved" (Acts 27:20 NIV). As their illusion of control dissolved, so did their hope. In a beautiful display of God's love, He assured Paul in a dream that he and his shipmates would not perish because He wanted him to stand trial before Caesar. Knowing the end of the story gave Paul a peace that sustained him through the rest of a journey in which nothing was within his control.

In the same way that God met Paul in a dream, God meets us in His Word, proclaiming that we should not attempt to control the "whens" and "hows" of our lives, but rather seek His kingdom (see Matthew 6:32–33).

Like Paul, you can experience peace in your storms because you know the end of the story—no matter what trials you encounter on earth, you will soon see Jesus face-to-face!

▶ **REFLECT** How have I seen God work when things were beyond my control?

▶ **PRAY** Father God, I confess that I often respond to fear by trying to control my circumstances and the people around me. Free me from my fear of the future with an eternal perspective and fill me with a peace that passes human understanding. I surrender, Lord; fulfill Your purposes for me.

▶ **DECLARE** God will fulfill His purposes for me.

▶ **ACT** Ask a trusted believer to share a time when they saw God work when things were out of their control.

85

Courage to Speak

> And because of my chains, most of the brothers and sisters
> have become confident in the Lord and dare all the more
> to proclaim the gospel without fear.
>
> Philippians 1:14 NIV

Imagine the leader of an infamous crime ring was caught and imprisoned. How would you expect the remaining gang members to respond? You'd probably think they would lie low for a while, taking time to regroup and recover.

Yet the arrest of key figures in the early Church had the opposite effect on their fellow believers. We hear of Paul's public punishment actually motivating others to become more vocal with the Good News of Jesus.

How do we explain this response to such a devastating setback? How could raised stakes only inspire greater risk-taking? Because these brothers and sisters did not have confidence in the response of their government, law enforcement or society. They had confidence in the Lord.

You do not need to be intimidated by the world's authority, or its view of the Gospel. God is able to advance His Kingdom within any circumstance, context or culture, even if it is hostile.

Be encouraged by the examples of believers before you who spread the Gospel without fear. When hindered, they did not back down. In this way, you can start to see "chains" as opportunities to lose confidence in the world and gain confidence in the Lord.

▶ **REFLECT** Where do I perceive "chains" around my ability to proclaim the Gospel today?

▶ **PRAY** Lord Jesus, I do not want to avoid proclaiming the Gospel because I am afraid of the consequences. Grant me the same courage You gave my brothers and sisters in the New Testament, to grow bolder in the face of attack. Help me value Your protection and approval above the world's. May Your kingdom come, no matter the cost.

▶ **DECLARE** God gives me courage to proclaim the Gospel.

▶ **ACT** Look up some testimonies from the persecuted Church today (see the Voice of the Martyrs' website, icommit topray.com) and pray for those believers.

86

Use Your Gifts

> For this reason I remind you to fan into flame the gift of
> God, which is in you through the laying on of my hands,
> for God gave us a spirit not of fear but of power and love
> and self-control.
>
> 2 Timothy 1:6–7 ESV

You have at least one supernatural gift from God meant to benefit the Church. If the weightiness of this responsibility makes you afraid, you are not alone.

The apostle Paul had laid hands on his spiritual son, Timothy, and Timothy had received the gift of evangelism. That gift was to help the Church grow by bringing others to Christ. Based on Paul's words in 2 Timothy 1:6–7, though, it appears that Timothy was hesitant to exercise his God-given gift, perhaps out of fear of failing at such an important task.

Paul reminded Timothy of both the Source of his gift (God) and the authority Timothy had in Christ to use his gift. As Paul showed Timothy, the courage to use our spiritual gifts comes from looking not to ourselves, but to the Giver of the gift.

Every Christian has at least one spiritual gift that comes about when the Holy Spirit works supernaturally in his or her life (see 1 Corinthians 12:7–10), and God wants us to use them to build up His people.

You don't have to fear imperfection or failure when you use your spiritual gifts, because it is the Holy Spirit who is working through you to fulfill God's will for the Church.

▶ **REFLECT** What spiritual gifts has God given me?

▶ **PRAY** Father, thank You for the gifts You have given me. I pray that if any spiritual gift You have given me has become cold, I will begin to rekindle it today. I pray that I will boldly and lovingly put my gifts to daily use without fear and that my mind will be directed by Your Spirit.

▶ **DECLARE** The Holy Spirit has given me gifts to bless the Church.

▶ **ACT** Use one of your spiritual gifts to bless another believer today. If you aren't sure what your spiritual gifts are, talk to a trusted spiritual leader or take a free online assessment.

87 Courageous Contentment

> Keep your life free from love of money, and be content with
> what you have, for he has said, "I will never leave you nor
> forsake you." So we can confidently say, "The Lord is my
> helper; I will not fear; what can man do to me?"
>
> Hebrews 13:5–6 ESV

Have you ever wanted more money? Ever longed for greater
security or stability in your life? Fear of lack is common in
the human experience and can lead you to look for many
different forms of relief and reassurance.

Jesus knows our concerns and offers us a simple cure:
Himself. In never leaving us, He becomes the basis for our
security. In never forsaking us, He becomes our guarantee
of help in any situation. His presence gives us access to
unlimited and uncorrupted resources.

By contrast, we are warned about loving money. This is
because we will inevitably crave more of it—but more cannot satisfy or save us, nor is more always possible. God's
promised presence might not increase your bank account
balance or eliminate hardship. But believing and speaking
it out *can* change your feelings and desires.

With the Lord as your Helper, you can be free from trusting in your job or finances. You can be free from worrying that certain people or circumstances might ruin you. You can enjoy what you have instead of fretting over what you don't have. You can live in the present—because of God's presence, with you and for you.

▶ **REFLECT** In what area do I need to look to the Lord for security rather than my finances?

▶ **PRAY** Lord, my Helper, I don't want to seek ultimate security in anything or anyone other than You. Increase my trust in You as my Provider and Protector. Satisfy my cravings for more money or things with Your presence. When I fear not having enough, remind me of Your promises. I want to rely fully and fearlessly on You.

▶ **DECLARE** The Lord is my Helper and my security.

▶ **ACT** Have a discussion with someone about all that you both have to be thankful for and in what ways you are content.

Going against the Flow

> Who is going to harm you if you are eager to do good? But
> even if you should suffer for what is right, you are blessed.
> "Do not fear their threats; do not be frightened."
>
> 1 Peter 3:13–14 NIV

Humility. Integrity. Compassion. Respect for others. According to studies, these are some of the top ten characteristics of highly admired people. Do you recognize these as values already commended and commanded in the Bible?

Peter's rhetorical question in this passage suggests a Christian in character and in action should not pose a problem. Most people want to make the world a better place. As partners with God in redemption, reconciliation and restoration, Christians ought to be well-received and well-regarded by others. We are not to make excuses or imagine opposition that simply isn't there.

Yet human definitions of "good" and "right" change with the times, shaped by the culture. God's goodness and rightness always expose sin and provoke attack from the enemy. The reality is, at any moment we may go from being admired to being antagonized. This is one cost of pursuing God's ways.

Whether refusing to be dishonest at work or upholding a conviction among friends, you may suffer for staying true to Christ. Although a natural reaction to opposition and threats is fear, stand firm, remembering that God is pleased by your commitment to His ways. To echo Peter's encouragement: Don't be scared, and keep on doing what you are doing.

▶ **REFLECT** In doing what is right, how have I been blessed?

▶ **PRAY** God, I am blessed whenever I do what is right and good according to You. Whether I am appreciated, threatened or actually harmed in the process, You stay with me and are for me. Help me continually turn from evil and pursue good. With You on my side, there is nothing and no one to be afraid of.

▶ **DECLARE** God gives me courage to do what is right.

▶ **ACT** Think of two ways to do good to someone: one you know will be appreciated and one that will involve uncertainty and risk. Ask God for courage to accomplish both.

89 | Courage in Suffering

"Do not fear what you are about to suffer. Behold, the devil is about to throw some of you into prison, that you may be tested, and for ten days you will have tribulation. Be faithful unto death, and I will give you the crown of life."

Revelation 2:10 ESV

If Jesus wrote your church a letter, what would it say? How would He comment on the way your community lives out their faith? Jesus' letter to the church in Smyrna shows the kind of faithfulness He looks for in His followers.

The book of Revelation contains messages from Jesus to a group of first-century churches. Revelation 2:10 addresses believers in Smyrna, where the trials brought on by following Jesus, which He alluded to throughout His ministry, are becoming reality. Jesus informs and affirms them—not so they can evade the suffering but endure it.

Most of us can only imagine being persecuted for our faith. Yet this verse indicates we should expect all kinds of tests as Christians, even death. Jesus understands that the idea of suffering can frighten us. While He does not always remove hardships, He promises never to forsake us and to reward our faithfulness with eternal life.

Does practicing your faith cost you on any level? If fears of being mistreated or misunderstood hold you back from fully expressing your commitment to Jesus, receive His encouragement today: He knows what is coming, He is with you and He makes any suffering for His sake worth it.

▶ **REFLECT** How do I feel about suffering for my faith?

▶ **PRAY** Jesus, Your compassionate message to those first believers inspires me. Help me apply Your words to my own walk today and release my fears of suffering to You. I want to faithfully follow You in tests, in trials, even in death. Your rewards are more precious than my own safety and comfort.

▶ **DECLARE** God is with me in persecution.

▶ **ACT** Consider any people who make you feel threatened or intimidated as a Christian and, guided by the Holy Spirit, prepare what you will say when you are shamed or persecuted.

Awestruck by His Glory

> When I saw him, I fell at his feet as if I were dead. But he laid his right hand on me and said, "Don't be afraid! I am the First and the Last. I am the living one. I died, but look—I am alive forever and ever! And I hold the keys of death and the grave."
>
> Revelation 1:17–18 NLT

When you are in awe, you feel respect or reverence mixed with dread and wonder, often inspired by something majestic or powerful. An encounter with God will leave you awestruck, but not afraid.

Although John was going through the worst time in his life, exiled to the island of Patmos for preaching his testimony about Jesus, he was worshiping in the Spirit when he had a face-to-face encounter with the Great I Am.

This encounter came with such dread and wonder, John fell down as if he was dead. He saw Jesus Christ, the Conqueror and victorious One, alive forever and holding the keys of death and the grave. And this eternal Conqueror gently laid His hand on John and told him not to be afraid. This personal encounter reveals how God wants us to be awestruck by His glory but not afraid.

When God's glory drives you to your knees in worship, Jesus responds to you as He did to John: He tells you not to fear because He is the One who willingly died in your place and now lives forever.

Fear not! Worship Him in the Spirit and be awestruck by the glory of the One who loves you.

▶ **REFLECT** When have I been awestruck by God's glory?

▶ **PRAY** Father God, I worship You with all my mind, soul and body today. Reveal Your glory, that I may stand in renewed awe of who You are and what You have done. Teach me how to worship You in the Spirit like John, especially during adverse times. I know You are reigning over my situation today and that You love me.

▶ **DECLARE** Jesus is alive forever and reigns over my life!

▶ **ACT** Do one of the following to meditate on God's glory: take a nature walk, listen to a worship song or swap stories with a friend about your experiences with God.

SPECIAL INVITATION

As you read this book, you may have realized that you want to go deeper in your relationship with God, or that you have yet to welcome Jesus into your life and follow Him as King.

In the beginning, God created the world, and everything was good (see Genesis 1–2). But after the first humans disobeyed God, sin entered the world, which separated us from God and brought eternal death (see Genesis 3; Romans 3:23, 5:12, 6:23).

The good news is that "God so loved the world, that he gave his only Son [Jesus], that whoever believes in him should not perish but have eternal life" (John 3:16 ESV). Jesus came to earth, lived a sinless life and was crucified, receiving the punishment for our sins. He rose from the dead, defeating sin and death, and will return as King.

Will you receive Jesus as your Lord and Savior? Share your heart with God in this prayer: *Jesus, I no longer want to do things my way, and I choose to follow You as my Lord. Forgive me and fill me with Your Holy Spirit to live for You every day.*

To discover resources to help you grow in your faith, visit

- Bible.com or the YouVersion Bible app
- Messengerx.com or the MessengerX app
- Faithful.co or the Faithful app
- Chosenbooks.com